MORE
ARTISTS OF THE RIGHT

by

K. R. BOLTON

EDITED BY GREG JOHNSON

Counter-Currents Publishing Ltd.
San Francisco
2017

Copyright © 2017 by K. R. Bolton
All rights reserved

Cover image: Franz von Lenbach, *Portrait of Richard Wagner*,
circa. 1882–83, Lenbachhaus, Munich

Cover design by Kevin I. Slaughter

Published in the United States by
COUNTER-CURRENTS PUBLISHING LTD.
P.O. Box 22638
San Francisco, CA 94122
USA
http://www.counter-currents.com/

Hardcover ISBN: 978-1-940933-19-1
Paperback ISBN: 978-1-940933-20-7
E-book ISBN: 978-1-940933-21-4

Library of Congress Cataloging-in-Publication Data

Bolton, K. R. (Kerry Raymond), 1956-
  More artists of the right / by K. R. Bolton ; edited by Greg Johnson.
    1 online resource.
  Includes index.
  Summary: "More Artists of the Right, K. R. Bolton's companion to his 2012 volume Artists of the Right, explores the work of seven artists who also made contributions to Right-wing political thought: composer and essayist Richard Wagner, occultist and poet Aleister Crowley, poet and critic T. S. Eliot, novelist and critic P. R. Stephensen, poet and essayist A. R. D. Fairburn, poet and essayist Count Potocki of Montalk, and novelist and essayist Yukio Mishima" -- Provided by publisher.
  Description based on print version record and CIP data provided by publisher; resource not viewed.
  ISBN 978-1-940933-21-4 (epub) -- ISBN 978-1-940933-19-1 (hardcover : alk. paper).
  Literature--20th century--History and criticism. 2. Fascism and literature. 3. Fascism and music. 4. Music--19th century--History and criticism. I. Johnson, Greg, 1971- editor. II. Bolton, K. R. (Kerry Raymond), 1956- Artists of the right. III. Title.

PN56.F35
809'.93358--dc23

2015010835

Contents

Foreword by Greg Johnson ❖ iii

1. Richard Wagner ❖ 1

2. Aleister Crowley ❖ 26

3. T. S. Eliot ❖ 44

4. P. R. Stephensen ❖ 79

5. A. R. D. Fairburn ❖ 103

6. Count Potocki of Montalk ❖ 129

7. Yukio Mishima ❖ 158

Index ❖ 175

About the Author ❖ 184

Foreword

It is a perennial embarrassment to the Left that some of the greatest creative minds of the 19th and 20th centuries were men of the Right, and not just conservatives, but men of the far Right, such as fascists and National Socialists—or their precursors and fellow travelers.

Kerry Bolton's *More Artists of the Right* offers political profiles of seven such artists: Richard Wagner, Aleister Crowley, T. S. Eliot, P. R. Stephensen, A. R. D. Fairburn, Count Potocki of Montalk, and Yukio Mishima. All seven were immensely accomplished artists and critics who made significant contributions to Right-wing political thought. Wagner is one of the most influential artists of all time. Eliot won the Nobel Prize in Literature. Mishima is one of the giants of 20th-century Japanese literature. Stephensen, Fairburn, and Potocki are best-known in Australia and New Zealand, but Bolton establishes that they deserve a much larger audience. Crowley and Stephensen's purely artistic productions are somewhat marginal to their bodies of work; although a prolific and accomplished poet as well as a novelist, Crowley is best known for his occult writings, whereas Stephensen is best known as an essayist and publisher.

The present volume is a companion to Bolton's 2012 volume *Artists of the Right: Resisting Decadence*, which focuses on ten leading 20th-century literary figures: D. H. Lawrence, H. P. Lovecraft, Gabriele D'Annunzio, Filippo Marinetti, W. B. Yeats, Knut Hamsun, Ezra Pound, Wyndham Lewis, Henry Williamson, and Roy Campbell. The chapters on Stephensen, Fairburn, and Mishima are much expanded versions of chapters originally published in *Thinkers of the Right: Challenging Materialism* (Luton, England: Luton Publications, 2003).

I wish to thank Kerry Bolton for his hard work, patience, and good humor over the long process of bringing this project to birth. I also wish to thank Collin Cleary, John Morgan, Michael Polignano, and Kevin Slaughter for all their help.

Greg Johnson
March 12, 2017

Chapter 1

Richard Wagner

Karl Marx reserved a special place of contempt for those he termed "reactionists." These comprised the alliance that was forming around his time among all classes of people, high-born and low, who aimed to return to a pre-capitalist society. These were the remnants of artisans, aristocrats, landowners, and pastors, who had seen the ravages of industrialism and money-ethics then unfolding. Where there had once been craft, community, village, the marketplace, and the church, there was now mass production, class war, the city, and the stock exchange.

Rather than deploring capitalism, as one might suppose, Marx regarded this as an indispensable phase in the "wheel of history," of the historical dialectic, which would through a conflict of thesis and antitheses result in a socialist and eventually a communist society. This was the inevitable unfolding of history according to Marx, based on a struggle for primacy by economic interests: class struggle, where primitive communism, feudalism, capitalism, socialism, and communism represented a linear progression. Hence, anything that interfered with this process was "reactionism."[1]

Capitalism itself would go through a stage of increasing internationalization and concentration, whereby increasing numbers of bourgeois would be dispossessed and join the ranks of the proletariat that would make a revolution to overthrow capitalism.[2] Hence, Marx sought to overthrow the traditions and ethos of pre-capitalist society. As "reactionary" historians such as Oswald Spengler[3] and Julius Evola[4] have pointed out, given

---

[1] Karl Marx, *The Communist Manifesto* (Moscow: Progress Publishers, 1975), pp. 46–47.

[2] *The Communist Manifesto*, pp. 41, 44.

[3] Oswald Spengler, *The Decline of the West* (London: George Allen and Unwin, 1971), Vol. II, pp. 402, 506.

that dialectics means that the new "synthesis" incorporates elements of what it has overthrown, Marxian-socialism was itself an aspect of capitalism.[5]

Marx came into a revolutionary milieu comprised of varying elements but which generally took inspiration from the French Revolution of 1789, with an emphasis on the "rights of man" that provided a reformist façade for the rise of the bourgeoisie. Hence these revolutionaries of the mid-19th century regarded themselves as "democrats" fighting for equality. However, they also saw the nation-state and the sovereignty of peoples as the liberating factor from princes, kings, dynasties, and empires that were seen as placing themselves above "the people." Hence, nationalism became the revolutionary force of the century, albeit at times intended, like Jacobinism, as a prelude to a "universal republic."

VOLK & NATION AS REVOLUTIONARY FORCES

The German Revolution moved in a *völkisch* direction, where the *Volk* was seen as the basis of the state, and the notion of a *Volk*-soul that guided the formation and development of nations became a predominant theme that came into conflict with the French bourgeois liberal-democratic ideals. J. G. Fichte had laid the foundations of a German nationalism in 1807–1808 with his *Addresses to the German Nation*. Like possibly all revolutionaries or radicals of the age, he started off under the impress of the French Revolution. However, by the time Fichte had delivered his addresses he had already rejected Jacobinism, and his views became increasingly authoritarian and influenced by the *Realpolitik* of Machiavelli.

Johann Gottfried Herder had previously sought to establish

---

[4] Julius Evola, *Men Among the Ruins* (Rochester, Vermont: Inner Traditions International, 2002), pp. 167–68.

[5] Cf. K. R. Bolton, *The Banking Swindle: Money Creation and the State* (London: Black House Publishing 2013), "The Real Right's Answer to Socialism and Capitalism," pp. 152–74 and K. R. Bolton, "Marx Contra Marx: A Traditionalist Conservative Critique of the *Communist Manifesto*," http://www.anamnesisjournal.com/issues/2-web-essays/43-kr-bolton

the concept of the *Volk*-soul, and of each nation being guided by a spirit. This was a metaphysical conception of race, or more accurately *Volk* (people, nation), that preceded the biological arguments of Count Arthur de Gobineau in his seminal treatise *The Inequality of the Human Races*, which was to impress Wagner decades later. Herder's doctrine is evident in Wagner's, insofar as Herder stated that the *Volk* is the only class, and includes both king and peasant, and that "the people" are not the same as the rabble heralded by Jacobinism and later by Marxism. Herder upheld the individuality and distinctness of nations that had fortuitously been separated by both natural and cultural barriers, and held that these nations manifested innate differences, including religious ones.

Wagner's rejection of French ideals in favour of Germanic ones, as one might expect, can be traced to aesthetic sensibilities, and his stay in Paris gave him a distaste for the "exaggerations" of French music.[6] In France Wagner was acquainted with Jews whom he came to distrust and said of this period that it had promoted his consciousness as a German:

> On the other hand, I felt strongly drawn to gain a closer acquaintance of German history than I had secured at school. I had Raumer's *History of the Hohenstaufen* within easy reach to start upon. All the great figures in this book lived vividly before my eyes. I was particularly captivated by the personality of that gifted Emperor Frederick II, whose fortunes aroused my sympathy so keenly that I vainly sought for a fitting artistic setting for them. The fate of his son Manfred, on the other hand, provoked in me an equally well-grounded, but more easily combated, feeling of opposition. . . .
>
> Even at this time it delighted me to find in the German mind the capacity of appreciating beyond the narrow bounds of nationality all purely human qualities, in how-

---

[6] Richard Wagner, *My Life*, Part I, http://www.wagneropera.net/MyLife/RW-My-Life-Part-1-1813-1842.htm

ever strange a garb they might be presented. For in this I recognised how nearly akin it is to the mind of Greece. In Frederick II, I saw this quality in full flower. A fair-haired German of ancient Swabian stock, heir to the Norman realm of Sicily and Naples, who gave the Italian language its first development, and laid a basis for the evolution of knowledge and art where hitherto ecclesiastical fanaticism and feudal brutality had alone contended for power, a monarch who gathered at his court the poets and sages of eastern lands, and surrounded himself with the living products of Arabian and Persian grace and spirit—this man I beheld betrayed by the Roman clergy to the infidel foe, yet ending his crusade, to their bitter disappointment, by a pact of peace with the Sultan, from whom he obtained a grant of privileges to Christians in Palestine such as the bloodiest victory could scarcely have secured.[7]

This seemingly universalistic ideal of "humanity" is however at the root of his suspicion of the Jews as possessing traits inimical to "humanity." Herder, Fichte, and other founders of German Idealism, including Kant, had taken the same view, their German nationalism including a certain universalism that saw the Germans as having a messianic world mission, just as the British, Jews, and Russians[8] have all held themselves to be bearers of a world mission vis-à-vis the whole of humanity. It was in Frederick however, that Wagner "beheld the German ideal in its highest embodiment." "If all that I regarded as essentially German had hitherto drawn me with ever-increasing force, and compelled me to its eager pursuit, I here found it suddenly presented to me in the simple outlines of a legend, based upon the old and well-known ballad of 'Tannhäuser.'"[9]

---

[7] *My Life*, Part I.
[8] British = a civilizing mission, Jewish = a domineering material mission, Russian = a metaphysical mission.
[9] *My Life*, Part I, op. cit.

THE DRESDEN REVOLT & BAKUNIN

Having returned to Dresden from Paris in 1842, Wagner secured a position as a conductor at the Royal Theatre, a profession that failed to enthuse him over the course of seven years. However, it was here that the arch-revolutionist of anarchism, the Russian noble, Mikhail Bakunin, despite being a fugitive, sat in the audience at the public rehearsal of Beethoven's Ninth Symphony conducted by Wagner, who wrote:

> At its close [Bakunin] walked unhesitatingly up to me in the orchestra, and said in a loud voice, that if all the music that had ever been written were lost in the expected world-wide conflagration, we must pledge ourselves to rescue this symphony, even at the peril of our lives. Not many weeks after this performance it really seemed as though this world-wide conflagration would actually be kindled in the streets of Dresden, and that Bakunin, with whom I had meanwhile become more closely associated through strange and unusual circumstances, would undertake the office of chief stoker.[10]

Wagner had met Bakunin in 1848, while the Russian was a fugitive from the Austrian authorities, in the house of a friend, the republican leader August Röckel. Wagner described the visage of Bakunin when they first met: "Everything about him was colossal, and he was full of a primitive exuberance and strength. I never gathered that he set much store by my acquaintance. Indeed, he did not seem to care for merely intellectual men; what he demanded was men of reckless energy."[11]

Bakunin looked to his fellow Slavs as what we might call the new barbarians, who could regenerate humanity, "because the Slavs had been less enervated by civilization."[12] He could cite Hegelian dialectics at length and was committed to the destruc-

---

[10] *My Life*, Part II, http://www.wagneropera.net/MyLife/RW-My-Life-Part-2-1842-50.htm

[11] *My Life*, Part II.

[12] *My Life*, Part II.

tion of the old order, and saw in the Russian peasant the best hope of starting a world conflagration. The destructive urge of the Russian giant bothered Wagner. Bakunin cared nothing for the French—although he had started his ideological journey by reading Rousseau, like many radicals of the time—nor for the ideals of republicanism or democracy. Wagner however, feared that such forces of destruction, once unleashed, would annihilate all culture, and that nothing could arise again:

> Was any one of us so mad as to fancy that he would survive the desired destruction? We ought to imagine the whole of Europe with St. Petersburg, Paris, and London transformed into a vast rubbish-heap. How could we expect the kindlers of such a fire to retain any consciousness after so vast a devastation? He used to puzzle any who professed their readiness for self-sacrifice by telling them it was not the so-called tyrants who were so obnoxious, but the smug Philistines. As a type of these he pointed to a Protestant parson, and declared that he would not believe he had really reached the full stature of a man until he saw him commit his own parsonage, with his wife and child, to the flames.[13]

While Bakunin was untempered fury, Wagner was a contemplative aesthete who was to ruminate for decades on revolution as a means to achieve a higher state of humanity. Ultimately, he influenced the course of history more so than his Russian friend.

Bakunin deplored Wagner's intention to write a tragedy entitled *Jesus of Nazareth*, and implored Wagner to make it a work of contempt towards a figure whom Bakunin regarded as a weakling, while Wagner saw in Jesus the figure of a hero. Indeed, Wagner, a pantheist and heathen who sought the redemption of man through returning to nature and overthrowing the superficiality of a decaying civilization, nonetheless admired Jesus as a revolutionary hero whose message was re-

---

[13] *My Life*, Part II.

demption from mammon. He was to state to the Dresden Patriotic Club in the revolutionary year of 1848 that God would guide the revolution against "this daemonic idea of Money ... with all its loathsome retinue of open and secret usury, paper-juggling, percentage and banker's speculations. That will be the full emancipation of the human race, that will be the fulfilment of Christ's pure teaching."[14]

Yet paradoxically, again Bakunin betrayed his own repressed aestheticism when he intently listened to Wagner play and sing *The Flying Dutchman* and applauded enthusiastically. Wagner saw in Bakunin a man conflicted with the "purest ideal of humanity" and "a savagery entirely inimical to all civilization." Wagner's ideal was "the artistic remodelling of human society." However, Wagner's fears subsided when he found that Bakunin's plans for destruction were as utopian as his own plans to reshape humanity through aesthetics. Also, for all his zeal, Bakunin had no real means or following.[15]

Bakunin was back with Wagner in 1849, after a brief sojourn to see if the Slavs could be incited, and it was in Dresden that both were involved in the city's revolt against the King of Saxony. Wagner on his own account felt no great attraction to democratic politics, but assumed the role of revolutionary it seems through a dissatisfaction with life: "My feelings of partisanship were not sufficiently passionate to make me desire to take any active share in these conflicts. I was merely conscious of an impulse to give myself up recklessly to the stream of events, no matter whither it might lead."[16]

Nonetheless, the German democratic revolution was seen by many, including Wagner, as the means of dismantling principalities for the purpose of creating a united German nation. It was where a dichotomy between the democratic and the *völkisch* revolutions arose, the first derived from French inspiration and Jewish intellectualism such as that of Heine, the second

---

[14] Cited by Paul Lawrence Rose, *Wager: Race and Revolution* (London: Faber and Faber, 1996),

[15] Rose, p. 52.

[16] Rose, p. 52.

from the roots of Germany, and expressed by Fichte, Hegel, and Herder.

Wagner had already issued a clarion call for "Revolution" in an essay by that name just prior to the May 1849 revolt in Dresden. Like Bakunin, his revolution was a call to instinct and to *vitalism*, antithetical to the intellectualism of Jewish socialists and democrats. It was a romanticism of revolt that sought the overthrow of states because they suppressed the instinct, the vitality of life that welled up from within the *Volk* soul. He saw revolution as a "supernatural force" and referred to it as "a lofty goddess." Wagner wrote: "I [the revolution] am the ever rejuvenating, ever fashioning Life." "Everything must be in a state of becoming." "Life is law unto itself."[17] Wagner's ode to vital forces had no kinship with the theoretical disputations of Marx.

Yet, Wagner's appeal was also to the kings and princes. He saw the ideal of the king as being the first among the *Volk*, and not as a debased hereditary ruler representing a single class. Wagner's idea of kingship harkened to the primeval Germans who selected their kings from among the populace on the basis of their heroism. Like Herder, Wagner saw the populous as one class, the *Volk*, and what Wagner was really fighting against was a system that intervened between *Volk* and king. Wagner wrote a *völkisch* appeal for princes and people to unite against the East, albeit unpublished, possibly because it did not express the sentiments of certain Jewish liberal publishers: "The old fight against the East returns again today. The people's sword must not rust / Who freedom wish for aye."[18] He wrote in an article published in the *Dresdener Anzeiger* on the intrinsic value of kingship, and posed the question as to whether all the issues debated by the democrats cannot nonetheless be met under the personage of the king?

---

[17] Wagner, "Revolution," cited by Peter Viereck, *Metapolitics: From Wagner and the German Romantics to Hitler* (New Brunswick, New Jersey: Transaction Publishers, 2004), p. 109.

[18] Viereck, p. 109.

I must own, however, that I felt bound to urge this king to assume a much more familiar attitude towards his people than the court atmosphere and the almost exclusive society of his nobles would seem to render possible. Finally, I pointed to the King of Saxony as being specially chosen by Fate to lead the way in the direction I had indicated, and to give the example to all the other German princes.[19]

What did inspire Wagner was the revolt in Vienna that had seen workers and students unite. Yet Wagner was repelled by the rhetoric and the demagoguery of the revolutionary movement, which he regarded as "shallow." It was the abhorrence of an aesthete who is instinctively repelled by the mob and its leaders.[20] Referring to the Dresden revolutionary committee of which he was a member, Wagner wrote that the part he played "as in everything else, was dictated by artistic motives."[21]

Wagner had made enemies of the court petty officials who surrounded the king. The pressure mounted to deprive Wagner of his position as conductor of the Royal Theatre in Dresden, although the king resisted those pressures, and Wagner assured himself that the king had understood him. After a short period in Vienna Wagner returned to Dresden, more concerned with "theatrical reform" than with social reform.

Around this time, however, Wagner's friend Röckel was released on bail from prison for his role in the revolutionary movement. Röckel began to publish a journal extolling the aims of the French anarchist Proudhon, to whose theories Wagner states he was completely converted. He regarded his aesthetic revolution as first requiring a cleansing revolt by the "socialists" and "communists." In this he as always sought to eliminate mammon from life, and to place humanity on an aesthetic foundation.

---

[19] *My Life*, Part II.
[20] K. R. Bolton, *Artists of the Right: Resisting Decadence*, ed. Greg Johnson (San Francisco: Counter-Currents, 2012), *inter alia*.
[21] *My Life*, Part II.

Proudhon, as Röckel explained to him,[22] advocated the elimination of the role of the middleman, which again meant the elimination of the role of the Jew, whom Proudhon described as a typical mercantile race, "exploiting," "anti-human," and "parasitic."[23] Indeed, many in the socialist movement, including even Jews such as Marx, saw the Jew as the eternal middleman and socialism as the means by which humanity, including the Jews themselves, could be emancipated from a money-god that had shaped the entirety of modern civilization. Marx expressed the attitude toward the Jews held by many in the Young Germany movement in his essay "On the Jewish Question":

> What is the secular basis of Judaism? *Practical* need, *self-interest*. What is the worldly religion of the Jew? *Huckstering*. What is his worldly God? *Money*. Very well then! Emancipation from *huckstering* and *money*, consequently from practical, real Judaism, would be the self-emancipation of our time. An organization of society which would abolish the preconditions for huckstering, and therefore the possibility of huckstering, would make the Jew impossible. His religious consciousness would be dissipated like a thin haze in the real, vital air of society. On the other hand, if the Jew recognizes that this *practical* nature of his is futile and works to abolish it, he extricates himself from his previous development and works for *human emancipation* as such and turns against the supreme practical expression of human self-estrangement. We recognize in Judaism, therefore, a general *anti-social* element of the *present time*, an element which through historical development — to which in this harmful respect the Jews have zealously contributed — has been brought to its present high level, at which it must necessarily begin to disintegrate. In the final analysis, the *emancipation of the Jews* is the emancipation of mankind from *Juda-*

---

[22] Rose, p. 29.
[23] Rose, p. 64.

ism. This is no isolated fact. The Jew has emancipated himself in a Jewish manner, not only because he has acquired financial power, but also because, through him and also apart from him, *money* has become a world power and the practical Jewish spirit has become the practical spirit of the Christian nations. The Jews have emancipated themselves insofar as the Christians have become Jews.[24]

Setting aside the fact that Marx himself was a huckster motivated by self-interest and the "God of money,"[25] it is important to note that these sentiments were the common outlook of German radicals in the milieu in which Wagner lived and worked. They were to be expressed in similar terms a decade later by Wagner himself in his essay "Judaism in Music," which has made him irredeemable in the eyes of many Jewish, Leftist, and liberal critics.

Wagner's friend Bakunin saw Marx and Rothschild as part of "a single profiteering sect, a people of bloodsuckers, a single gluttonous parasite . . ."[26] Bakunin, started his career as a revolutionary with the Young Hegelians in Germany, with an article published in one of their journals in 1842, entitled "Reaction in Germany." What Bakunin advocated for his fellow Slavs was a federated Slavic republic stretching across Europe, on the ruins of the Hapsburg melting-pot. Non-Slavic minorities would live under Slavic rule.

His grandiose aim did not find favor at the Congress of Slavic Nationalities that he attended in Prague in 1848. He appealed for collaboration among German, Hungarian, and Slavic radicals. He hoped for simultaneous revolts in Bohemia, Hungary, and the German states. Paradoxically, what the chief pro-

---

[24] Karl Marx, "On the Jewish Question," February, 1844 in *Deutsch-Französische Jahrbücher*; http://www.marxists.org/archive/marx/works/1844/jewish-question/

[25] K. R. Bolton, *The Psychotic Left* (London: Black House Publishing, 2013), pp. 70–100.

[26] Michael Bakunin, 1871, *Gesammelte Werke*, Band 3 (Berlin 1924), pp. 204–16.

ponent of anarchism sought was a totalitarian authority and the suppression of "all manifestations of gabbing anarchy" across the federated Slav bloc. Such were the ideals of a current of the European revolution which fought side-by-side with Jewish intellectuals, neo-Jacobins, and bourgeois democrats, most of whom, for one reason or another, regarded the nation-state or the *Volk* as the means of securing freedom against dynasties and empires.

Bakunin's internationalism was but a phase that begun with the founding of the *Internationale* in 1864 and ended with his disillusionment with the "masses" in 1874; his internationalist-anarchism had comprised merely ten years of his life.[27] At the time of his friendship with Wagner, as they walked about Dresden in tumult, with Prussian troops advancing, Bakunin was a Pan-Slavic anti-Semite.

On May 1, 1849, the Chamber of Deputies of Saxony was dissolved, and Röckel, having been a Deputy, now lost his legal immunity. Wagner supported Röckel in the continuation of his journal, *Volksblatt*, which also provided a meagre income for Röckel's family. While Röckel escaped to Bohemia, revolution broke out in Dresden, as Wagner busily worked on *Volksblatt*. It was in his position as a journalist that Wagner observed the revolutionary proceedings and the loss of control of the bourgeois liberal theorists to the mob. On May 3 bells rang out from St. Anne's church tower as a call to take up arms. On Wagner's account, he seems to have been driven by the enthusiasm of the moment. He recounts that he looked on as though watching a drama unfold until, caught up with the zeal of the crowd, he transformed from spectator to actor:

> I recollect quite clearly that from that moment I was attracted by surprise and interest in the drama, without feeling any desire to join the ranks of the combatants. However, the agitation caused by my sympathy as a

---

[27] Max Nomad, *Apostles of Revolution* (Boston: Little, Brown and Company, 1939), "The Heretic: Michael Bakunin: Apostle of 'Pan-Destruction.'"

mere spectator increased with every step I felt impelled to take.[28]

While the King of Saxony and his government and officials fled, the King of Prussia ordered his troops to march on Dresden. At this time news reached Dresden that an uprising had taken place at Württemberg, with the support of the local soldiery. Wagner saw the prospect of an invasion from Prussia as an opportunity to appeal to the patriotic sentiments of the Dresden soldiers, and *Volksblatt* presses came out with an appeal in bold type: "Seid Ihr mit uns gegen fremde Truppen?" (Are you on our side against the foreign troops?). The appeal was ineffective. The initial attitude of Bakunin, who emerged from his hiding place to causally wander about the barricades, smoking a cigar and deriding the amateurism of the revolutionary efforts, was that the revolt was chaotic, and he saw no point in remaining to support the doomed insurrection. However, a provisional government was formed, while news was coming from all around Germany that other cities were in revolt.[29]

On May 6, the Prussian troops fired on the market square. The heroic actions of a single individual who remained, unarmed, atop the barricades while everyone fled, rallied the defenders, and they thwarted the Prussian advance. This heroism was now enough for Bakunin to throw in his lot with the revolt. The revolt lasted a few weeks, before which Wagner had already left Dresden, and started making arrangements for the performance of *Tannhäuser* at Weimar.

Wagner's participation in the revolt seems to have been primarily as a propagandist, and he, like Bakunin, did not see much substance in it. While Bakunin was inspired by an individual act of heroism, Wagner had been enthused by the sight of a well-formed people's militia on the march: the forerunner of a regenerated *Volk*.

Wagner was regarded as one of the primary leaders of the

---

[28] *My Life*, Part II.
[29] *My Life*, Part II.

revolt and fled to Switzerland and from there to Paris. Here again he become acquainted with the Jews as middlemen in the music world, whom he had come to distrust previously in that city. He then went back to Zurich, where he wrote the pamphlets *Kunst und Revolution* (Art and Revolution) and *Das Kunstwerk der Zukunft* (The Artwork of the Future). Back in Paris, Wagner started writing for a German radical journal, for which he prepared a lengthy essay, "Art and Climate," and then went back to Zurich.[30]

With the support of many German aristocrats and other well-placed individuals, Wagner returned to Germany via Weimar. In 1863, after petitioning Saxony, he was amnestied and permitted to resettle in Dresden.[31]

Those who see Wagner "selling-out" his socialist principles for the sake of royal patronage fail to understand that his "socialism" was not some type of class struggle for the rule of the proletariat, but was for a unified *Volk* from out of which would emerge a Hero-King-Redeemer. He maintained his closeness to many princes and princesses, counts and countesses, until finally securing the patronage of King Ludwig of Bavaria.[32]

"COMMUNISM": *GEMEINSAMKEIT*

In 1849, Wagner was still alluding to a universalistic creed that co-existed uneasily with the sentiments of the German *völkisch* freedom movement, having a few years earlier written of "love for Universal Man."[33] That same year, however, he was articulating a conception of art that was thoroughly *völkisch*. In *The Art-Work of the Future*, Wagner explains the *völkisch* basis of art, and in so doing the intrinsically "socialist" character of art not as an expression of the artist's ego, but the artist as expressing the *Volk*-soul.

Ultimately his ideas were pantheistic and heathen, seeing

---

[30] *My Life*, Part II.

[31] *My Life*, Part IV, http://www.wagneropera.net/MyLife/RW-My-Life-Part-4-1861-1864.htm

[32] *My Life*, Part IV.

[33] Richard Wagner, *Art and Climate*, 1841, p. 264, http://users.belgacom.net/wagnerlibrary/prose/wagclim.htm

nature as the basis of human action, and the artificial civilization that had subjugated nature as the object for revolt: "The real Man will therefore never be forthcoming, until true Human Nature, and not the arbitrary statutes of the State, shall model and ordain his Life; while real Art will never live, until its embodiments need be subject only to the laws of Nature, and not to the despotic whims of Mode."[34]

Part III of his essay is devoted to "The Folk and Art," which in his essay on "Revolution and Art" just shortly before, is made subsidiary to the "universal man." The *Volk* now assumes the central role as the "vital force." The *Volk* were all those, regardless of class, who rejected ego and considered themselves part of a "commonality."[35] The subversion of this is the desire for "luxury," and the subordination of the state and the *Volk* to capital, industry and the machine.

This alienation of man from Nature, observed Wagner, leads to "fashion," where the "modern artist" creates a "freshly fangled fashion," or "a thing incomprehensible," by resorting to "the customs and the garb of savage races in new-discovered lands, the primal fashions of Japan and China, from time to time usurp as 'Mannerisms,' in greater or in less degree, each several departments of our modern art."[36]

It is with socialism or "communism" that Wagner repudiated the great enemy of the art of the future: the individual alienated from the *Volk*. What is translated into English as "communism" was rendered in German as *Gemeinsamkeit*,[37] meaning "commonality," hence we can discern something quite different between Wagner's "communism" and what is today understood as "communism."

It was not until several decades later that Wagner seems to have concluded that the folk should be a stable unit rather than a phase along the evolution to "Universal Man," and that the

---

[34] Richard Wagner, *The Art-Work of the Future*, 1849, p. 72, http://users.belgacom.net/wagnerlibrary/prose/wagartfut.htm
[35] *Art-Work of the Future*, Chapter I, Part III.
[36] *Art-Work of the Future*, Part V, p. 88.
[37] *Art-Work of the Future*, Part V, p. 147.

reality of racial differences made societies in constant flux due to external circumstances undesirable. Influenced by his friend Count de Gobineau, who made race a physical rather than a metaphysical issue, Wagner explained in his essay "Hero-dom and Christendom" that racial mixing among "noble" and "ignoble" races results in the irredeemable fall of the noble. For Wagner, the noblest of all races was the "white." Now Wagner wrote that the "uniform equality" of humanity, which he had once dreamt of as evolving into "Universal Man" under the leadership of the free German, "is unimaginable in any but a horrifying picture."[38]

In 1850 Wagner published *Judaism in Music*, an important treatise in understanding his revolutionary ideas. Since the distinct characteristics of an object can be most clearly understood by comparing it with another object, the character of the German *Volk* was most evident by comparing it with the perceived traits of the Jews in their midst. Wagner alludes to this in a later essay, when stating that one can most readily state what is "German" by comparison with what is Jewish.[39] *Judaism in Music* was also the treatise that marked Wagner as a seminal leader of modern German "anti-Semitism" as a forerunner of National Socialism.

As noted, Wagner's views on Jews were fairly typical of the ideologues of German Idealism, and of anti-capitalist radicals such as Proudhon, Bakunin, and Marx, the common belief being that Jews had detached themselves from "humanity," and that the liberation of humanity from Jewishness would also emancipate the Jews.

As Wagner explained in *Judaism in Music*, he is only concerned with the Jews in culture rather than in politics or religion. As far as politics goes, with reference to Herr Rothschild as being "Jew of the Kings" rather than being content as "King of the Jews," Wagner referred to the former "liberalism" of

---

[38] Richard Wagner, "Hero-dom and Christendom," 1881, http://users.belgacom.net/wagnerlibrary/prose/waghero.htm

[39] Richard Wagner, "What is German," 1876, http://users.belgacom.net/wagnerlibrary/prose/wagwiger.htm

himself and his fellow radicals as "a not very lucid mental sport," that failed to understand the true character of the *Volk*. Likewise, for all the radicals' declarations on emancipating the Jews in theory, there remained an instinctive revulsion in practice.

So far from needing emancipation, the Jew "rules, and will rule, so long as Money remains the power before which all our doings and our dealings lose their force."[40] Hence, being the middleman and the moneychanger, Jewish influence in the arts turns culture into an "art-bazaar." While Wagner could still talk of the "Universal Man," he nonetheless also refers in 1850 to something "disagreeably foreign" about the Jew no matter to which European nationality he belongs. While speaking the language of the nation in which he dwells, he nonetheless "speaks it always as an alien."

Wagner had just a year previously written of *Volk* communities as subjected to change as per external circumstances, as a natural and desirable historical development, but here writes of a community as an enduring historical bond, and not as "the work of scattered units." This is a development from his prior anarchistic definitions of communities as pragmatic rather than enduring: "only he who has unconsciously grown up within the bond of this community, takes also any share in its creations."[41]

The Jew however has developed as a people, "outside the pale of any such community,' as "splintered, soilless stock" whose communal attachment is to their God Jehova. Hence, the Jewish contribution to music, vocally, has been "a creaking, squeaking, buzzing snuffle," "an intolerably jumbled babbler." It is modern society based on money that has emancipated the Jew and therefore brought the Jew into the arts.

By 1850 then, Wagner had largely disposed of any former universalistic ideals, in favor of a *völkisch* doctrine. Over the next few decades, having recognized the folly of previous types

---

[40] Richard Wagner, *Judaism in Music*, 1850, p. 82, http://users.belgacom.net/wagnerlibrary/prose/wagjuda.htm

[41] *Judaism in Music*, p. 85.

of radicalism, he had fully embraced a *völkisch* ideology that remained rooted wholly in his first calling as an artist. Wagner's ideal remained the elevating of humanity, led by the Germans, to higher levels of Being, of that which defines what is *human*, towards man-as-artist manifesting his creativity and appreciation for creativity within the context of the *Volk* community. Hence, the following year he wrote of his transcendence of the current *isms*: "I am neither a republican, nor a democrat, nor a socialist, nor a communist, but—an artistic being; and as such, everywhere that my gaze, my desire, and my will extend, an out-and-out revolutionary, a destroyer of the old by the creation of the new."[42]

His aesthetic ideals did not temper his zeal for revolution, but enhanced them, writing to a friend, "the bloodiest hatred for our whole civilization, contempt for all things deriving from it, and longing for nature . . . only the most terrific and destructive revolution could make our civilized beasts 'human' again."[43]

His "anarchism" was the type of the free Germanic *Volk* who did not tolerate tyrants and whose concept of "freedom" was that of communal, *Volk* freedom, and not the egotism of the individual, a type of "anarchism" nonetheless that was postulated by Bakunin and later by Kropotkin, that states that communities are organically formed by free association from instinct, and not imposed by laws. "The same Wagnerian spirit favouring in music the revolt of emotional inspiration against classical rules favours in politics the revolt of instinctive *Volk* against law," writes Peter Viereck.[44] By 1865 he had repudiated the widespread revolutionary spirit of 1848, as "a Jewish importation of French rationalism," Viereck states.[45] Wagner explained his rejection of the prior era of revolt, writing in 1876 that:

---

[42] Rose, p. 177.
[43] Rose, p. 177.
[44] Viereck, p. 108.
[45] Viereck, p. 109.

I have no hesitation about styling the subsequent revolutions in Germany entirely un-German. "Democracy" in Germany is purely a translated thing. It exists merely in the "Press," and what this German Press is, one must find out for oneself. But untowardly enough, this translated Franco-Judaico-German Democracy could really borrow a handle, a pretext and deceptive cloak, from the misprised and maltreated spirit of the German Folk. To secure a following among the people, "Democracy" aped a German mien; and *"Deutschthum,"* "German spirit," "German honesty," "German freedom," "German morals," became catchwords disgusting no one more than him who had true German culture, who had to stand in sorrow and watch the singular comedy of agitators from a non-German people pleading for him without letting their client so much as get a word in edgewise. The astounding unsuccessfulness of the so loud-mouthed movement of 1848 is easily explained by the curious circumstance that the genuine German found himself; and found his name, so suddenly represented by a race of men quite alien to him.[46]

While critics claim that Wagner reneged on his former revolutionary ideas to curry favor with the aristocracy, his greatest patron being King Ludwig of Bavaria, his great English admirer, the Germanophilic English-born philosopher, Houston Stewart Chamberlain, who married Wagner's daughter Eva, said of the maestro that he remained a revolutionist from 1840 to the day of his death, on the basis that you cannot separate corrupt society from corrupt art.[47]

Wagner's revolutionary "freedom" was the innate German instinct for freedom; not the French, nor the English nor the Jewish conceptions of humanism and liberalism, of freedom for commerce and for parliaments. That *völkisch* freedom could as well be served in the ancient institution of a King if that King

---

[46] Wagner, *What is German*, p. 167.
[47] Cited in Viereck, p. 109.

embodied the *völkisch* spirit. The Wagnerian leader is a nexus with the divine and the highest embodiment of the *Volk*. Wagner referred to the leader who would liberate the Germans as the *Volk* itself, in contrast to a class of money interests. He called the *Volk* a "hero," the "folk-king" and the legendary "Barbarossa." The *Volk* was the German King Arthur who awakens from a slumber when his people are most endangered. Wagnerians looked for the Germanic Messiah, the re-born Barbarossa as the saviour of Germany.

Even in 1848 Wagner sought a King who would embody the *Volk*; a King who would be "the first of the *Volk*" and not merely representative of a class, and he sought to elevate the King of Saxony to that position, rather than to overthrow him.[48] He was a "republican" in a very definite sense, not of wishing to overthrow the King, but of the king leading the *res publica*, the public — the people — the *Volk* — as a unitary whole. Such a "folk-king" must transcend class and selfish interests. Here we see that Wagner could have no time for the banalities of parliament or of class war. Such matters as parliaments, constitutions, and parties were divisive to the *völkisch* organism, undermined the authority of the folk-king, and reduced the *Volk* to separate constituents rather than maintaining a unitary organic state.[49]

However Wagner drew a distinction between king and monarch, because a monarch is a member of a hereditary class who does not arise from the *Volk*. Indeed, we see how monarchies might disintegrate over centuries, where they are based on birth rather than achievement. Birth-lineage often becomes degenerate and effete, perhaps with no recourse other than through revolution, which more generally throws up a rulership that is worse. Wagner looked to the primeval Germanic kingship drawn from selection among free men, which was the rule of *Herodom*, the divine Hero[50] who often figures in the plot of his operas.

In his essay "Art and Revolution," Wagner introduced his

---

[48] Viereck, pp. 111–12.
[49] Viereck, p. 112. Viereck calls all of this "monstrous sophistries."
[50] Richard Wagner, *Bayreuther Blatter*, September 1881.

remarks by an admission of his own muddled thinking at the time of the Dresden revolt. He sought to amalgamate the ideas of Hegel, Proudhon, and Feuerbach into a revolutionary philosophy. "From this arose a kind of impassioned tangle of ideas, which manifested itself as precipitance and indistinctness in my attempts at philosophical system."[51]

Not wishing to be misunderstood as a supporter of the Parisian Commune (as was then frequently supposed), Wagner explains that his use of the term "communism" refers to the repudiation of "egos." By "communism" he means the collectivity of the *Volk*, "that should represent the incomparable productivity of antique brotherhood, while I looked forward to the perfect evolution of this principle as the very essence of the associate Manhood of the Future." This Germanic conception was antithetical to the Jacobin, liberal-democratic mind of the French.[52] He regarded Germany as having a mission among the nations, by virtue of a "German spirit," to herald a new dawn of creativity that renounced egotism and the economics that was driven by it.[53] Quoting Thomas Carlyle[54] on the epochal impact of the French Revolution and the "'spontaneous combustion' of humanity," Wagner saw this mission of the German race as one of creation rather than destruction, and the "breaking out of universal mankind into Anarchy."[55] In "Art and Revolution," Wagner addressed the question of the impact of the late 1840s European revolt on the arts, and where the artist had been in the era preceding the tumult. It was the "Hellenic race," once overcoming its "Asiatic birthplace," which gave rise to a "strong manhood of freedom," most fully expressed in their god Apollo, who had slain the forces of Chaos, to bring forth "the fundamental laws of the Grecian race and nation." In Greece, including Sparta, art and state and war-craft were an

---

[51] Richard Wagner (1849) "Art and Revolution," in *The Art-Work of the Future*, Vol. 1, 1895, p. 26.

[52] "Art and Revolution," p. 29.

[53] "Art and Revolution," p. 30.

[54] Thomas Carlyle, *History of Frederick II of Prussia*, http://www.gutenberg.org/files/25808/25808-h/25808-h.htm

[55] "Art and Revolution," p. 30.

organic unity.⁵⁶ The Athenian "spirit of community" then fell to "egoism" and split itself along "a thousand lines of egoistic cleavage."⁵⁷ The degradation of the Roman world succumbed to "the healthy blood of the fresh Germanic nations," whose blood poured into the "ebbing veins of the Roman world." But art had sold itself to "commerce." Mercury, the God of commerce, had become the ruler of "modern art."

> This is Art, as it now fills the entire civilised world! Its true essence is Industry; its ethical aim, the gaining of gold; its aesthetic purpose, the entertainment of those whose time hangs heavily on their hands. From the heart of our modern society, from the golden calf of wholesale Speculation, stalled at the meeting of its cross-roads, our art sucks forth its life-juice, borrows a hollow grace from the lifeless relics of the chivalric conventions of mediaeval times, and—blushing not to fleece the poor, for all its professions of Christianity—descends to the depths of the proletariat, enervating, demoralising, and dehumanising everything on which it sheds its venom.⁵⁸

In ancient Greece, by contrast, art belonged to the entire populace, not to a single class. The contrast between Greek and modern education shows the differences between a *Volk* and a society of classes educated for commerce:

> The Greeks sought the instruments of their art in the products of the highest associate culture: we seek ours in the deepest social barbarism. The education of the Greek, from his earliest youth, made himself the subject of his own artistic treatment and artistic enjoyment, in body as in spirit: our foolish education, fashioned for the most part to fit us merely for future industrial gain, gives us a ridiculous, and withal arrogant satisfaction with our own

---

⁵⁶ "Art and Revolution," p. 33.
⁵⁷ "Art and Revolution," p. 36.
⁵⁸ "Art and Revolution," p. 43.

unfitness for art, and forces us to seek the subjects of any kind of artistic amusement outside ourselves . . .[59]

The task was not to restore the Greek tradition or anything else from the past, but to create new art, freed from commerce:

> From the dishonouring slave-yoke of universal journeymanhood, with its sickly Money-soul, we wish to soar to the free manhood of Art, with the star-rays of its World-soul; from the weary, overburdened day-labourers of Commerce, we desire to grow to fair strong men, to whom the world belongs as an eternal, inexhaustible source of the highest delights of Art.[60]

Only the "mightiest force of revolution"[61] can overthrow the money despotism and inaugurate the free "republic" where the whole populace partakes of the art that expresses its spirit. This however, was not a revolution of "the windy theories of our socialistic doctrinaires," who sought to level and proletarianize until there is no possibility of art. The aim was not universal proletarianization, as per Karl Marx, but what Wagner called "artistic manhood, to the free dignity of Man,"[62] emancipated from the economic treadmill.

BAYREUTH AS THE CENTER OF THE GERMAN REVOLUTION

Wagner's redemption of humanity, having found a patron in Ludwig of Bavaria, became centred on Bayreuth, where Wagner's pageants could be performed and a journal published (the *Bayreuther Blätter*) that would articulate the political and aesthetic ideals implicit in those operas. Wagner proceeded with a metapolitical strategy decades before the Italian Communist theorist Gramsci formulated his strategy of the "long march through the institutions," and subtly redirecting a socie-

---

[59] "Art and Revolution," p. 48.
[60] "Art and Revolution," p. 55.
[61] "Art and Revolution," p. 55.
[62] "Art and Revolution," p. 57.

ty by first changing its culture.[63]

> These ideas, together with the racial doctrines of de Gobineau, were intended to permeate German society, emanating from a cultural and metapolitical center, Bayreuth, intended as the microcosm of a *völkisch* classless society. The festival house at Bayreuth was what Wagner's son-in-law Chamberlain called in 1900 "a standard for armed warriors to rally around" in their revolt against corruption.[64]

Under the Second Reich of Bismarck, Bayreuth became a center of pilgrimage for those seeking "what Wagner's *Meistersinger* chorus calls 'the holy German art.'" The Second Reich relied on Bayreuth to give it an historical and mythic cult connecting the Golden Age of Frederick Barbarossa with that of Bismarck. Without Bayreuth the Bismarckian Reich would have been nothing more than a Prussian state edifice. Wagner Societies throughout Germany propagated the ideas emanating from Bayreuth.

Houston Stewart Chamberlain, whose racial history[65] championed the Holy Grail of Germandom and was expounded mystically in Wagner's operas, was the direct link between Wagner and the Third Reich. It seems likely that Wagner would have viewed with enthusiasm the mass parades of armed *Volk*, the purging of the arts, the breaking of usury, and the mantle of virtual kingship assumed by a war veteran who rose from the people.

As we have seen, whether Wagner's views are explicitly the doctrinal antecedent for National Socialism *per se* is questionable. His views on race and Jews were quite typical of revolutionaries of the time, including those of non-Germans such as

---

[63] Steven Yates, "Understanding the Culture War," http://www.lewrockwell.com/yates/yates24.html

[64] Viereck, p. 115.

[65] Houston Stewart Chamberlain, *Foundations of the Nineteenth Century* (London: John Lane Company, 1911).

Proudhon and Bakunin. History has been kinder to these than to Wagner because, despite their revolutionary *political* commitment, and Wagner's primary commitment to the arts, it was Wagner who has been the greater influence on history, attesting to the greater influence of the metapolitical over the political.

Counter-Currents/*North American New Right*
May 20, 2013

CHAPTER 2

ALEISTER CROWLEY

Aleister Crowley (1875–1947), who styled himself the "Great Beast 666," is an enduring presence both in the occult subculture and in contemporary popular culture. He is hailed by some as a philosopher, magician, and prophet. He is condemned by others as a depraved egomaniac. But, for the most part, he is merely consumed for his shock value and eccentricities.

Crowley belongs in a collection on "artists of the Right" because he was also both a prolific poet and novelist, as well as a social and political theorist who addressed the problems of industrialism, democracy, and the rise of mass man and society. Crowley's social and political theory is grounded in a Nietzschean critique of morality and a metaphysical critique of modernity that often parallels the Traditionalism of René Guénon and Julius Evola.

The influence of Nietzsche is evident in Crowley's aim of creating a new religion that would replace the "slave morality" inherent in the "Aeon of Osiris," represented in the West as Christianity. A new Aeon of "force and fire," the Aeon of Horus, "the Crowned and conquering child," would be built on a new "master morality." This was to be expressed in Crowley's new religion of "Thelema," a Greek word meaning "Will," understood in Nietzschean terms as "Will to Power": an endless upward striving to higher forms, both individual and collective.

CROWLEY & TRADITIONALISM

It may be surprising to group Crowley with Evola and Guénon as part of the counter-current to the leveling creeds of materialism, rationalism, and liberalism. Crowley, after all, is generally thought to have emerged from initiatic societies like Freemasonry and the Illuminati that promoted liberal humanism as a new "rationalist" religion, much as communism became a religion with its own saints, martyrs, holy wars, dogmas, rituals, and liturgies, despite its materialistic intentions.[1] Crowley, for instance, included Adam Weishaupt, founder of the Illuminati, in his list of "saints" for his Thelemite Gnostic Mass.[2] The vast bulk of Crowley's followers, moreover, are liberal humanists.

Guénon used the term "counter-tradition" to refer to attempts to promote liberalism and materialism in the guise of Tradition.[3] In the words of the well-known 19th-century authority on occultism Eliphas Lévi,[4] a former Freemason[5] and socialist propagandist turned Catholic:

> Masonry has not merely been profaned but has served as the veil and the pretext of anarchic conspiracies. . . . The anarchists have resumed the rule, square, and mallet, writing upon them the words Liberty, Equality, Fraternity — Liberty, that is to say, for all the lusts, Equality in degradation, and Fraternity in the work of destruction. Such are the men whom the Church has condemned justly and will condemn forever.[6]

To this day, the French Revolutionary slogan "Liberty, Equality, Fraternity" is the motto of the French Grand Orient lodge of Freemasons. These anti-initiatic secret societies were

---

[1] Note, for example, the embalming of Lenin and his entombment at an edifice reminiscent of the stepped pyramids of ancient priest-kings.

[2] Aleister Crowley, *Magick* (York Beach, Maine: Samuel Weiser, 1984), p. 430.

[3] René Guénon, *The Reign of Quantity & the Signs of the Times* (Ghent, New York: Sophia Perennis, 2002).

[4] Pen name for Alphonse Louis Constant.

[5] Lévi makes an allusion to having taken the oath of the "Rosy Cross," indicating he had been initiated into the quite high degree of Rosicrucian in Freemasonry. Eliphas Lévi, *The History of Magic* (London: Rider, 1982), p. 286.

[6] Eliphas Lévi, p. 287.

engaged in an occult war, with political, social, moral, and economic manifestations.

But this is not the whole story.

Even within these Masonic and illuminist movements, genuine occultists sought a return to the mythic and the re-establishment of the nexus between the earthly and the divine.[7] Pre-eminent among them was the Hermetic Order of the Golden Dawn in Britain, where Crowley entered his magical apprenticeship. The Golden Dawn was closely associated with Freemasonry, but it seems likely that its leaders, such as MacGregor Mathers and William Wynn Westcott, identified with a Traditionalist and un-profaned form of Masonry.[8] W. B. Yeats' membership in the Golden Dawn also counts as evidence of a Traditionalist current (even though Yeats was in bitter conflict with Crowley).

Surprisingly, Evola himself concedes that Crowley was, at least in part, a genuine initiate. Evola claims that the Golden Dawn was "to some extent" a successor "to those [orders] of an initiatic character."[9] Evola also granted that Crowley's system of *"magick"* was drawn from traditional initiatic practices: "It is certain that in Crowleyism the inoculation of magico-initiatic applications is precise, and the references or orientations of ancient traditions are evident."[10]

Given that Evola was writing of Crowley at a time when the

---

[7] Julius Evola, *Revolt Against the Modern World* (Rochester, Vermont: Inner Traditions, 1995).

[8] In this writer's opinion, Freemasonry is all a bunch of scabrous bastardy, which should be treated with suspicion, whether in its Grand Orient, "irregular," or United Grand Lodge forms. Westcott, founder of the Golden Dawn, for example regarded the "true religion" of Freemasonry to be Cabbalism. R. A. Gilbert, *The Magical Mason: Forgotten Hermetic Writings of William Wynn Westcott, Physician and Magus* (Northamptonshire: The Aquarian Press, 1983), Westcott, "The religion of Freemasonry illuminated by the Kabbalah," ch. 21, pp. 114–23.

[9] Julius Evola, "Aleister Crowley," trans. Cologero Salvo, http://www.counter-currents.com/2010/08/aleister-crowley/

[10] Evola, "Aleister Crowley."

world was in political ferment, and Evola was himself very much involved with that ferment as a critical supporter of Fascism, it is notable that even Evola did not explore the social and political implications of "Crowleyism," especially given that Crowley's expressed views were largely in accord with Evola's.[11]

Crowley, therefore, despite some of his associations, should not be counted among the counter-tradition. "Liberty, Equality, Fraternity" were repugnant to him, and it was frankly absurd for him to enroll Weishaupt[12] among the Thelemite "saints." Crowley's inclusion of Weishaupt can perhaps best be explained not in terms of what he was for, but in terms of what he was against. For Weishaupt directed much of his conspiratorial energy against the Catholic Church, which on a very superficial level might have prompted Crowley's admiration.

The initiatic Tradition championed by Evola and Guénon is fundamentally and frankly elitist and aristocratic. In Traditional society, "magick" was an integral part of life, a means of harmonizing human life with the cosmos. Thus, there is no foundation for equality and democracy, as Lévi writes:

> Affirmation rests on negation; the strong can only triumph because of weakness; the aristocracy cannot be manifested except by rising above the people. . . . The weak will ever be weak . . . the people in like manner will ever remain the people, the mass which is ruled and which is not capable of ruling. There are two classes: freemen and slaves; man is born in the bondage of his passions, but he can reach emancipation through intelligence. Between those who are free already and those who are as yet not there is no equality possible.[13]

---

[11] The most comprehensive examination of Evola's political and social views available in English translation is *Men Among the Ruins*, (Rochester, Vermont: Inner Traditions, 2002).

[12] John Robison, *Proofs of a Conspiracy* (Boston: Western Islands, 1967).

[13] Eliphas Lévi, *The History of Magic* (London: Rider, 1982), p. 44.

Crowley rejected democracy for the same reasons as Lévi, Evola, and Guénon. In his *Thelemic "Bible" The Book of the Law* (*Liber Legis*), Crowley writes of democracy: "Ye are against the people, O my chosen,"[14] about which Crowley commented: "The cant of democracy condemned."[15]

Having rejected democracy and other mass movements as innately alien to the "Royal Art," Crowley sought to develop the political and social aspects of Thelema, writing an uncharacteristically clear commentary on his 'bible,' *The Law is for All: An Extended Commentary on the Book of the Law*.

THE BOOK OF THE LAW

After Crowley predictably fell out with the leadership of the Golden Dawn, he spent several years traveling. In 1904 he and his wife Rose were in Egypt, where, according to Crowley, an event occurred that was of "Aeonic" significance. Crowley claims to have received a scripture for the "New Aeon," channeled from the "Gods" through a supernatural entity called Aiwass from whom Crowley claimed to have received *The Book of the Law* via automatic writing.[16] What was written by Crowley over the course of three days became the bible of Thelema, which *The Book of the Law* proclaims as the name of the doctrine.[17]

The Book of the Law reads in parts like a mystical rendering of Nietzsche, with a strident rejection of herd doctrines including Christianity and democracy. (Crowley lists Nietzsche as a

---

[14] Crowley, *Liber Legis* ("The Book of the Law") (York Beach, Maine: Samuel Weiser, 1976), 2: 25.

[15] Crowley, *The Law is for All* (Phoenix: Falcon Press, 1985), p. 192.

[16] Crowley was also, however, to call Aiwass his own "Holy Guardian Angel," or in mundane psychological terms his unconscious; therefore *Liber al Legis* could be regarded as an example of automatic writing, a likely explanation given that the writing styles of Aiwass and Crowley are remarkably similar.

[17] For an account of Crowley's occult career and the so-called "Cairo Working" where *Liber al Legis* was written, see Colin Wilson, *Aleister Crowley: The Nature of the Beast* (Wellingborough, Northamptonshire: The Aquarian Press, 1987).

"saint" in his Gnostic Mass.[18])

Under Thelema all doctrines and systems that restrict the fulfillment of the "will" or the "True Will," whether social, political, economic, or religious, are to be replaced by the Crowleyite religion of a new aeon, the Aeon of Horus, "The Conquering Child."[19] "Will" is the basis of Nietzschean evolution, and it becomes clear that Crowley was attempting to establish a Western mystical system of self-overcoming along the lines of ancient yogic practices of self-overcoming to achieve higher states of being.

"Do what thou wilt" is the foundation of Thelema.[20] It does not mean a nihilistic "do what you want," but "do your will" that is, your "true will," which must be discovered by rigorous processes. Crowley states that the dictum "must not be regarded as individualism run wild."[21] Reflecting the individual "true will," Thelemic doctrine describes "every man and every woman [as] a star."[22] That is, each individual is a part of the cosmos but with his or her own orbit,[23] or what one might call an individual life-course.

The Book of the Law states, "the slaves shall serve."[24] Again this is Nietzschean in the sense that many individuals, probably the vast majority, do not have the will to discover and fulfill their "true will." While everyone is a "star," some shine brighter than others. In *The Star Sponge Vision*,[25] an astral revelation, Crowley explained this inequality as reflecting the "highly organized structure of the universe" which includes stars that are of

---

[18] Crowley, *Magick*, p. 430.

[19] Part 3 of *Liber Legis* is the revelation of Horus as the God of the New Aeon, which aeonically follows that of Isis (matriarchy), and the present Aeon of Osiris, the religions of the sacrificial god, including Christianity. Horus is described as the god of war and vengeance. (*Liber Legis* 3:3).

[20] "There is no law beyond do what thou wilt." *Liber Legis* 3: 60.

[21] Crowley, *The Law is for All*, p. 321.

[22] *Liber Legis*, 1: 3.

[23] *The Law is for All*, pp. 72–75.

[24] *Liber Legis* 2: 58.

[25] Crowley, *The Law is for All*, pp. 143–45.

"greater magnitude and brilliance than the rest."[26] The mass of humanity whose natures are servile and incapable of what Nietzsche called "self-overcoming"[27] will remain as they are, their true wills being to serve the followers of a "master morality."[28] *The Book of the Law* describes these latter as "Kings of the Earth," those whose starry wills are those of rulers.[29] (If some of the prose supposedly dictated to Crowley by Aiwass sounds remarkably similar to Eliphas Lévi, it might be because Crowley claimed to be reincarnated from, among many sages from ancient to recent times, Lévi himself![30])

Such a doctrine, while individualistic, is not anarchic, nihilistic, or even liberal. It is, in fact, a revival of *castes*. More is implied here than mere *classes*, which are an economic and materialistic debasement. Castes reflect a metaphysical order in which each individual fulfils his function according to his true will — or duty, *dharma* — as manifestation of the cosmic order. To followers of the Perennial Tradition, caste is a manifestation of the divine order and not merely an economic division of labor for crass exploitation.[31]

Crowley (or Aiwass) explains the fundamental anti-democratic and anti-egalitarian doctrine of Thelema in the following terms, again reminiscent of Nietzsche:

> We are not for the poor and sad: the lords of the earth are our kinsfolk. Beauty and strength, leaping laughter, and delicious languor, force and fire are of us . . . we have

---

[26] Crowley, *The Law is for All*, pp. 143–45

[27] Friedrich Nietzsche, *Thus Spake Zarathustra* (Harmondsworth, Middlesex: Penguin Books, 1969), pp. 136–38.

[28] "There is a master morality and slave morality . . ." Nietzsche, *Beyond Good and Evil* (Middlesex: Penguin Books, 1984), p. 175.

[29] *Liber Legis* 2:58.

[30] *Magick*, p. 430. Other "Thelemic saints" listed in the Gnostic Mass from whom Crowley claimed to be reincarnated included Mohammed and Swinburne. Thankfully, Weishaupt is not among the lineage.

[31] Evola, *The Hermetic Tradition* (Rochester, Vermont: Inner Traditions, 1995), pp. 89–100.

nothing to do with the outcast and unfit. For they feel not. Compassion is the vice of kings; stamp down the wretched and the weak: this is the law of the strong; this is our law and the joy of the world.[32]

This hierarchical social order, while in accord with the perennial Tradition, postulates a *new* aristocracy, the old having become debased and beholden to commerce. (Crowley himself was of bourgeois origins, so he ennobled himself with the title of "Sir Aleister Crowley."[33]) Under the "Aeon of Horus"[34] the new aristocracy would consist of Nietzschean self-overcomers. Crowley specifically refers to the influence of Nietzsche in explaining the Thelemic concept: "The highest are those who have mastered and transcended accidental environment. . . . There is a good deal of the Nietzschean standpoint in this verse."[35]

However, in contrast to Nietzsche as well as Guénon and Evola, Crowley also draws on Darwinism. After referring to the "Nietzschean standpoint" Crowley states in Darwinian terms:

It is the evolutionary and natural view . . . Nature's way is to weed out the weak. This is the most merciful way too. At present all the strong are being damaged, and their progress being hindered by the dead weight of the weak limbs and the missing limbs, the diseased limbs and the atrophied limbs. The Christians to the lions.[36]

Crowley saw an era of turmoil preceding the New Aeon during which the masses and the elite, or the new aristocracy, would be in conflict. Crowley wrote of this revolutionary prelude to the New Aeon: "And when the trouble begins, we aristocrats of freedom, from the castle to the cottage, the tower or the

---

[32] *Liber Legis* 2: 17–21.
[33] Crowley, *Magick*, "Gnostic Mass," "The Saints," p. 430.
[34] "I am the Hawke-headed god of silence and of strength." (*Liber Legis* 3: 70).
[35] *The Law is for All*, p. 175.
[36] *The Law is for All*, p. 175.

tenement, shall have the slave mob against us."[37]

Crowley describes "the people" as "that canting, whining, servile breed of whipped dogs which refuses to admit its deity . . ."[38] The undisciplined mob at the whim of its emotions, devoid of Will, is described as "the natural enemy of good government." The new aristocracy of governing elite will be those who have discovered and pursued their "true will," who have mastered themselves through self-overcoming, to use Nietzsche's term. This governing caste would pursue a "consistent policy" without being subjected to the democratic whims of the masses.[39]

THE THELEMIC STATE

The form of Thelemic government is vaguely outlined in *The Book of the Law*, suggesting a type of corporatism: "Let it be the state of manyhood bound and loathing: thou hast no right but to do what thou will."[40] Contrary to the anarchic or nihilist interpretation often given Thelema's "do what thou wilt," Crowley defined the Thelemic state as a free association for the common good. The individual will is accomplished through social cooperation. Individual will and social duty should be in accord, the individual "absolutely disciplined to serve his own, and the common purpose, without friction."[41]

Crowley clarified his meaning so as not to be confused with anarchism or liberalism. Although his *Liber Oz* (stating the "rights of man")[42] seems to be a formula for total individual sovereignty devoid of social restraint, Crowley wrote that it must not be interpreted as advocating unfettered individualism.[43]

In what might appear to be his own effort at a "papal encyclical" on good government, Crowley explains:

---

[37] *The Law is for All*, p. 192.
[38] *The Law is for All*, p. 192.
[39] *The Law is for All*, p. 193.
[40] *Liber Legis*, 1: 42.
[41] *The Law is for All*, p. 101.
[42] *The Law is for All*, p. 321, *Liber Oz*.
[43] *The Law is for All*, p. 321

I have set limits to individual freedom. For each man in this state which I propose is fulfilling his own True Will by his eager Acquiescence in the Order necessary to the Welfare of all, and therefore of himself also.[44]

Crowley's rejection of democracy and all that might be termed "slave morality"[45] necessitated a new view of the state. Like others of his time, including fellow mystics such as Evola and Yeats,[46] Crowley was concerned with the future of culture under the reign of mercantilism, materialism, and industrialism. He feared that an epoch of mass uniformity was emerging. He saw equality as the harbinger of uniformity, again appealing to biology:

There is no creature on earth the same. All the members, let them be different in their qualities, and let there be no creature equal with another. Here also is the voice of true science, crying aloud: "Variety is the key of evolution." Know then, O my son, that all laws, all systems, all customs, all ideals and standards which tend to produce uniformity, being in direct opposition to nature's will to change and develop through variety, are accursed. Do thou with all thy might of manhood strive against these forces, for they resist change which is life, and they are of death.[47]

This biological rather than metaphysical approach was supported by reference to human differences caused by "race, climate and other such conditions. And this standard shall be based upon a large interpretation of Facts Biological."[48]

---

[44] Crowley, *The Book of Wisdom or Folly* (York Beach, Maine: Samuel Weiser, 1991), clause 39, *Liber Aleph Vel*, CXI.
[45] Nietzsche, *Beyond Good and Evil* (Harmondsworth, Middlesex: Penguin Books, 1991), p. 175.
[46] K. R. Bolton, *Thinkers of the Right* (Luton: Luton Publications, 2003).
[47] *The Law is for All*, p. 228.
[48] *The Law is for All*, p. 228.

Referring to the passage in *The Book of the Law* that states "Ye are against the people, O my chosen!"[49] Crowley explained:

> The cant of democracy condemned. It is useless to pretend that men are equal: facts are against it. And we are not going to stay dull and contented as oxen, in the ruck of humanity.[50]

The democratic state as a reflection of equality and thus of uniformity was to be replaced by what is often termed the "organic state" or the "corporative state." This conception may be viewed both biologically, as in the organism of the body (hence "corporatist") with the separate organs (individuals, families, crafts, etc.) functioning according to their own nature while contributing to the health of the whole organism (society). The state assumes the authority of the "brain" as the co-coordinating organ of the separate parts. In England, corporatism was called "guild socialism," among the Continental Left "syndicalism."

Corporatism also had a metaphysical aspect, as the basis of social organization in Traditional societies, including the guilds of Medieval Europe and the corporations of ancient Rome. In Traditional societies, guild or corporatist social organization was, like all else, seen as a terrestrial manifestation of the cosmic order, the divine organism, and castes were primarily spiritual, ethical, and cultural organs, as distinct from the economic "classes" of debased secular societies. Hence, Evola advocated corporatism as the Traditionalist answer to class society.[51]

Crowley's conception of an organic state is described in *De Ordine Rerum*:

> In the body every cell is subordinated to the general physiological Control, and we who will that Control do not ask whether each individual Unit of that Structure be consciously happy. But we do care that each shall fulfill its

---

[49] *Liber Legis* 2: 25
[50] *The Law is for All*, p. 192.
[51] Evola, *Men Among the Ruins*, pp. 224–34.

Function, with Contentment, respecting his own task as necessary and holy, not envious of another's. For only mayst thou build up a Free State, whose directing will shall be to the Welfare of all.[52]

Hence Crowley, far from being a misanthrope, was concerned with freeing individuals from being part of a nebulous mass, and with providing sustenance for their material and cultural well-being as far as their natures allowed. The deliberate cultivation of his image as "evil" must be viewed primarily as a perverse quirk, and in particular a result of his twisted sense of humor, his narcissistic personality, and his strict upbringing among the Plymouth Brethren. He was delighted to have a mother who called him the Anti-Christ, which seems to have had a lasting effect on his thoughts and deeds throughout his life.

Crowley addressed himself to a major problem for unorthodox economic and social theorists, that of the reduction of working hours when a new economic system had secured physical abundance for all, and freed humanity from the economic treadmill. Once the obligations to the social order had been met, there should be "a surplus of leisure and energy" that can be spent in pursuit of individual satisfaction.[53] A sufficient amount of leisure time free from strictly material pursuits is the basis of culture, and the flowering of culture in the Medieval era, for example, was a product of this, coupled with a spiritual basis for society.

Crowley, like the Social Creditors and certain non-Marxian socialists or social reformers, wished to change the economic system in order to reduce working hours. His comments about the role of money are astute. Like the Social Creditors, Crowley believed that a change in the role of money is necessary for transforming the social and economic system. He was certainly aware of A. R. Orage's *New Age* magazine, where the minds of Social Creditors, guild socialists, and literati met. (Crowley re-

---

[52] *The Law is for All*, pp. 251–52.
[53] *The Law is for All*, p. 230.

ferred to the journal in another context in his autobiography.[54]) He rather perceptively set out his economic and financial policy as follows:

> What IS money? A means of exchange devised to facilitate the transaction of business. Oil in the engine. Very good then: if instead of letting it flow as smoothly and freely as possible, you baulk its very nature; you prevent it from doing its True Will. So every "restriction" on the exchange of wealth is a direct violation of the Law of Thelema.[55]

Once the material welfare of the citizen is secured, then the energy expended on economic necessities can be turned to the pursuit of culture. Under the Thelemic state the citizen would be directed by the ruling caste to pursue the higher aspects of life leading to the flowering of culture: "And because the people are oft-time unlearned, not understanding pleasure, let them be instructed on the Art of Life."[56] From this regime would follow a high culture in which each citizen would have the capacity to participate or at least appreciate: "These things [economic welfare] being first secured, thou mayst afterward lead them to the Heavens of Poesy and Tale, of Music, Painting and Sculpture, and into the love of the mind itself, with its insatiable Joy of all Knowledge."[57]

Under the Thelemic state every individual would be given the opportunity to fulfill his true will. Crowley maintained, however, that most true wills or "stars" would be content with a satisfying material existence, having no ambition beyond "ease and animal happiness," and would thus be content to stay where they are in the hierarchy. Those whose true will was to pursue higher aims would be given opportunities to do so, to "establish a class of morally and intellectually superior men and

---

[54] Crowley, *The Confessions of Aleister Crowley* (London: Routledge & Kegan Paul, 1986), p. 544.
[55] Crowley, *Magick Without Tears* (Arizona: Falcon Press, 1983), p. 346.
[56] *The Law is for All*, p. 251.
[57] *The Law is for All*, p. 251.

women." In this state, while the people "lack for nothing," their abilities according to their natures would be utilized by the ruling caste in the pursuance of a higher policy and a higher culture.[58]

Crowley also addressed the problem of industrialization and the role of the machine in the process of dehumanization, or what might also be termed by Traditionalists *desacralisation*,[59] a problem that continues to confront the post-industrial world with greater challenges than ever:

> Machines have already nearly completed the destruction of craftsmanship. A man is no longer a worker, but a machine-feeder. The product is standardized; the result, mediocrity. . . . Instead of every man and every women being a star, we have an amorphous population of vermin.[60]

Consistent with his advocacy of an organic state and with the re-sacralization of work as craft, Crowley expounded the guild as the basis of a Thelemic social organization. The guild was the fundamental unit of his own esoteric order, Ordo Templi Orientis (OTO):

> Before the face of the Areopagus stands an independent Parliament of the Guilds. Within the Order, irrespective of Grade, the members of each craft, trade, science, or profession form themselves into a Guild, making their own laws, and prosecute their own good, in all matters pertaining to their labor and means of livelihood. Each Guild chooses the man most eminent in it to represent it before the Areopagus of the Eighth Degree; and all disputes between the various Guild are argued before that Body, which will decide according to the grand principles of the Order. Its decisions pass for ratification to the Sanctuary of the Gnosis,

---

[58] *The Law is for All*, p. 227.
[59] Evola, *Men Among the Ruins*, p. 224.
[60] Crowley, *The Law is for All*, p. 281.

and thence to the Throne.⁶¹

This guild organization for the OTO thus represents society as a microcosm as the ideal social order that Crowley would have established under a Thelemic regime: "For, in True Things, all are but images one of another; man is but a map of the universe, and Society is but the same on a larger scale."⁶²

Crowley's description is in every respect a succinct blueprint for the corporatist state, hierarchically ascending from each self-governing profession to a "parliament of guilds." It was the type of system much discussed and making ground as an alternative to capitalism and Marxism, advocated from sundry quarters from Evola and D'Annunzio, to syndicalists, to Catholic traditionalists, and embryonically inaugurated under Mussolini. Ironically from a Crowleyan perspective, Dollfuss's Austria and Salazar's Portugal embraced corporatism as an application of Catholic social doctrine.

Crowley calls the mass of people under his system of governance "the Men of the Earth" who have not yet reached a stage of development to participate in government, and would be represented before the kingly head of state by those who are committed to service.⁶³ The governing caste comprises a Senate drawn from an Electoral College,⁶⁴ those individuals committed to service through personal "renunciation," including the renunciation of property and wealth, having taken a "vow of poverty."⁶⁵ Of course the universal franchise has no place in the selection of Thelemic government:

> The principle of popular election is a fatal folly; its results are visible in every so-called democracy. The elected man is always the mediocrity; he is the safe man, the sound

---

[61] Crowley, *Liber CXCIV*, "O.T.O. An Intimation with Reference to the Constitution of the Order," paragraph 21, *The Equinox*, vol. III, no. 1, 1919.
[62] "An Intimation," paragraph 1.
[63] "An Intimation," paragraph 5.
[64] "An Intimation," paragraph 9.
[65] "An Intimation," paragraph 30.

man, the man who displeases the majority less than any other; and therefore never the genius, the man of progress and illumination.[66]

The Electoral College is selected by the king from volunteers who must show acumen in athletics and learning, a "profound general knowledge" of history and the art of government and a knowledge of philosophy.[67]

This corporatist and monarchical system was designed to "gather up all the threads of human passion and interest, and weave them into a harmonious tapestry . . ." reflecting the order of the cosmos.[68]

The Italian poet and war veteran D'Annunzio might have come closest to the Thelemite ideal with his short-lived Free City of Fiume, a regime governed by the arts that attracted numerous rebels, from anarchists and syndicalists to nationalists.[69] Crowley does not mention D'Annunzio in his autobiography, even though Crowley was in Italy in 1920, and D'Annunzio's enterprise ended in December of that year.[70]

As for the Italian Fascists, Crowley wrote: "For some time I had interested myself in *Fascismo* which I regarded with entire sympathy even excluding its illegitimacy on the ground that constitutional authority had become to all intents and purposes a dead letter."[71] Crowley saw the *Fascisti* in a characteristically poetic way, describing the blackshirts patrolling the railway as "delightful." "They had all the picturesqueness of opera brigands." As for the "March on Rome," Crowley stated that he thought the behavior of the *Fascisiti* "admirable."

Crowley quickly became disillusioned, however, and came to regard Mussolini as a typical *politico* who compromised his principles for popular support. The mass nature of Fascism caused

---

[66] "An Intimation," paragraph 10.
[67] "An Intimation," paragraph 12 and 13.
[68] "An Intimation," concluding remarks.
[69] Anthony Rhodes, *The Poet as Superman – D'Annunzio* (London: Weidenfeld & Nicolson, 1959).
[70] Rhodes, p. 221.
[71] Crowley, *Confessions*, p. 911.

suspicion among many of the literati who had originally supported it, such as Wyndham Lewis and W. B. Yeats. Crowley observed developments in Rome for three days, and was disappointed with Mussolini's compromises with the Catholic Church, which Crowley regarded as Mussolini's "most dangerous foe."[72] Of course such criticisms are common among observers of events rather than participants. Critics from afar can afford the luxury of theorizing without having to test their theories, and themselves, in the practicalities of office.

Crowley moved to Cefalu where he established his "Abbey of Thelema" in a ramshackle house. The death of follower Raoul Loveday resulted in Crowley's expulsion from Italy in 1923, by which time he had become an embarrassment to the Fascist regime.[73] However, one eminent individual who must have discerned a proto-fascist element in Thelema, before himself becoming one of the more significant spokesmen of Sir Oswald Mosley's British fascism, was J. F. C. Fuller, who achieved fame as the architect of modern tank warfare and as a military historian. Fuller was one of Crowley's earliest devotees, having first heard of him in 1905. Like Crowley, he was a Nietzschean with occult interests who regarded socialism as a leveling creed: "the scum on the democratic cauldron." His opposition to Christianity was likewise Nietzschean.[74]

Fuller met Crowley in London in 1906 and wrote Crowley's first biography, *The Star in the West*, which was the winner (and only entrant) of a competition to promote Crowley's poetry. Although Fuller's interest in the occult and mysticism was lifelong, he broke with Crowley in 1911, embarrassed by Crowley's escapades that drew blazing headlines from the tabloid press.

In 1932, Fuller was still writing in Nietzschean terms of socialism and democracy as products of Christianity. Joining the British Union of Fascists and becoming Mosley's military adviser, Fuller remained a lifelong Mosleyite, even after the Second

---

[72] Crowley, *Confessions*, p. 911.
[73] Wilson, *Aleister Crowley: The Nature of the Beast*, p. 133.
[74] Anthony Trythall, *Boney Fuller: The Intellectual General* (London: Cassell, 1977).

World War, but refused any further contact with Crowley.

While Fascists (particularly "clerical-fascists"), guild socialists, Social Creditors, Distributists, syndicalists *et al.* attempted to resolve the problems of the machine age, and Evola offered something of a practical plan in his *Men Above the Ruins*, Crowley's Thelemic social conceptions remained as otherworldly as his mysticism, and few of his followers seem to have given much attention to the political implications or implementation of Thelema.

Crowley, a poet and a mystic, not an agitator or a politician, had his own conception of historical cycles, albeit somewhat limited, in which the Aeon of Horus, the new age of "force and fire," would emerge with Crowley as its prophet. Just as Marx assured us that the victory of communism was the end of an inexorable historical process, Crowley thought the Thelemic world order would arise as a product of cosmic law. And just as Marx called upon socialists to become active agents of this historical process, Crowley envisioned that the ordeals demanded by his Holy Order would give rise to Thelemic Knights who would wage *jihad* against all the old creeds:

> We have to fight for freedom against oppressors, religious, social or industrial, and we are utterly opposed to compromise, every fight is to be a fight to the finish; each one of us for himself, to do his own will, and all of us for all, to establish the law of Liberty. . . . Let every man bear arms, swift to resent oppression . . . generous and ardent to draw sword in any cause, if justice or freedom summon him.[75]

Counter-Currents/*North American New Right*
September 2 & 3, 2010

---

[75] *The Law is for All*, p. 317

CHAPTER 3

T. S. ELIOT

The First World War brought to a climax a cultural crisis in Western Civilization that had been developing for centuries: money overwhelmed tradition, as Spengler would have put it[1] (or, to resort to the language of Marx, the bourgeoisie supplanted the aristocracy).[2] Industrialization accentuated the process of commercialization, with its concomitant urbanization and the disruption of organic bonds and social cohesion. This has thrown societies into a state of perpetual flux, with culture reflecting that condition.

It was — and is — a problem of the primacy of Capital. Marx is the most well-known supposed opponent of Capital, to which many of the literati turned (especially in the aftermath of the Great War). Others, however, turned to the Right and rejected capitalism not only on the basis of economics, but more importantly by rejecting the *Zeitgeist* of Capital of which Marxism was merely a reflection rather than an alternative. Among these latter were T. S. Eliot, one of the most influential luminaries of contemporary English literature.

Thomas Stearns Eliot was born in St. Louis Missouri in 1888. He attended Harvard University, Merton College, Oxford, and the Sorbonne. Like Ezra Pound, the New Zealand poets Rex Fairburn and Geoffrey Potocki de Montalk, and many others on the colonial peripheries of European civilization, Eliot sought out whatever was left of the cultural epicenter and settled in England in 1915, becoming a naturalized British subject in 1927.

---

[1] Oswald Spengler, *The Decline of The West*, trans. Charles Francis Atkinson (London: George Allen & Unwin, 1971), Vol. 2, p. 506.

[2] K. Marx and F. Engels, *The Communist Manifesto* (Moscow: Progress Publishers, 1975), p. 57. K. R. Bolton, "Reading Marx Right: A Reactionary Interpretation of the Communist Manifesto," http://www.counter-currents.com/2017/03/reading-marx-right/.

Eliot's choice to settle in England and become a naturalized Briton gets at the heart of the crisis of European culture, and of alienation. Peter Ackroyd—despite his conventionalism and lack of insight in summing up Eliot's concern about advancing barbarism—does provide some rare insight on the cultural alienation that was felt by Eliot and others:

> To what territory or tradition did he belong is another question, and one in which he himself found it difficult to resolve: in a letter to Herbert Read he remarked how he . . . did not believe himself to be an American at all. He was a "resident alien". . . .
>
> His sense of being an alien in America was by no means unique, however. Ezra Pound used much the same terms to describe his own position in the United States — he was, he said, brought up in a place with which his forebears had no connection. But they were not simply aliens in one community or another; they were estranged from the country itself. They grew up in a time of great ethical and social confusion—the intercontinental railways were changing the shape of the country, just as the vast tide of immigrants from southern and eastern Europe was radically reforming the ideas of what an "American" was. This was a society which fostered no living or coherent tradition, a society being created by industrialists and bankers, and by the politics and the religion which ministers to them, for those who feel themselves to be set apart, and who have found in their reading of literature a sense of life and of values not available to them in their ordinary lives, there is a terrible emptiness at such a time . . . the consequence was that Pound and Eliot—and also near contemporaries . . . sought to create traditions of their own . . .[3]

Since then, the "cultural pessimism" that arose in the aftermath of World War I has shown itself to be realism, and the

---

[3] P. Ackroyd, *T. S. Eliot* (London: Hamish Hamilton, 1984), pp. 24–25.

world has become "America" under the impress of what is overtly promoted as "globalization." Money and standardization reign supreme. The traditionalist has few recourses other than self-exile and isolation or seeking out like company in fringe movements. However, for Eliot and Pound, Europe still offered opportunities.

Taking employment as a schoolteacher, and then with Lloyds Bank in the City, Eliot's first published volume of verse was *Prufrock* in 1917. *The Waste Land* followed in 1922. He was by then an established literary figure: in 1922 he founded the small but influential literary journal *The Criterion*, and was appointed Director of Faber & Faber, the publishing house, a position which he retained throughout his life. In 1936, *Collected Poems 1909–1935* was published.

As a playwright his works include *Murder in the Cathedral* (1935), *The Family Reunion* (1939), *The Cocktail Party* (1950), *The Confidential Clerk* (1954), and *The Elder Statesman* (1959). A book of verses for children, *Old Possum's Book of Practical Cats*, was published in 1939.

Eliot was also a renowned critic. A collection of his essays and reviews was published in 1920, entitled *The Sacred Wood*. *Selected Essays* appeared in 1932; *The Use of Poetry and the Use of Criticism* in 1933, *What is a Classic?* in 1945; *On Poetry and Poets* in 1957; *Poetry and Drama* in 1951; and *The Three Voices of Poetry* in 1953. In particular, Eliot's social and political criticism is found in *After Strange Gods* (1934), based on a lecture to the University of Virginia in 1933; *The Idea of a Christian Society* (1939); and *Notes Towards the Definition of Culture* (1948). These three essays are particularly cogent expressions of Eliot's criticism of liberalism and commercialism and his apologia for tradition.

In 1948, Eliot was awarded the Order of Merit and the Nobel Prize in Literature, followed by many honorary doctorates, honorary fellowships, and professorships in Britain and the United States. Although nothing deterred Eliot's lifelong criticism of liberalism and defense of tradition, and despite the continuing occasional quips about "anti-Semitism," and "racism," Eliot managed to avoid the opprobrium and persecution that was meted out to his friend Ezra Pound. He never compromised his views in a post-1945 world in which democracy and egalitarianism had assumed idolatrous veneration.

Eliot's turn to the Right was based on what has been called "cultural pessimism," represented in particular by the historical doctrine of Oswald Spengler, who saw cultural decay as part of an all-encompassing cycle of decline of Western civilization. Fritz Stern called this "the politics of cultural despair" in his study on the intellectual and cultural critique of liberalism in Weimar Germany.[4] Eliot's cultural pessimism and his quest for solutions was reflected in his personal crises, expressed in early poems, in particular "The Hollow Men" and "The Waste Land." The poet here becomes a microcosm of the crisis of culture as a whole. Having considered Eliot's personal ups and downs, Alastair Hamilton nonetheless calls him a social commentator of substance, who remained "reasonable" in his critique of modern industrial society.[5]

SOCIAL CREDIT: AN ECONOMIC SOLUTION TO CULTURAL PROBLEMS

However, there was a practical solution that attracted Eliot, as it did in particular Ezra Pound. The new economic theory of Social Credit provided a practical scheme for eliminating the social dislocations caused by an economic system founded on usury. In addition, it had the advantage, from a traditionalist viewpoint, of eliminating the prospect—which then seemed imminent—of a Bolshevik revolution intent on destroying the social order from which high culture emerges, whatever the Left-wing intelligentsia might say otherwise.

In particular, Social Credit provides the practical mechanism for overthrowing the money power which, according to Spengler, rules in the late epoch of a civilization, and apparently without the Spenglerian recourse to bloodshed and the rise of a fascistic "Caesar" figure.

---

[4] F. Stern, *The Politics of Cultural Despair: A Study in the Rise of the Germanic Ideology* (New York: Anchor Books, 1965).

[5] A. Hamilton, *The Appeal of Fascism: A Study of Intellectuals & Fascism* (New York: The Macmillan Co., 1971).

While few of the Right-wing literati concerned themselves with such practical details (most were *aesthetic* Rightists by and large), it is significant that the primary advocate of Social Credit, aside from Maj. C. H. Douglas, was A. R. Orage, editor of *The New English Review* and *The New Age* and one of the most important promoters of new literary talent. Although Orage was a luminary of the Fabian socialist movement, he was not an orthodox socialist and advocated guild-socialism.

Orage was a focus for both innovative art and innovative economic and social theories, and a few of the poets saw the importance of Social Credit as the means of overthrowing materialism. In particular there was Ezra Pound, a lifelong enthusiast for the doctrine, who was also Eliot's patron in London. It was Pound who enabled Eliot to get published in both Britain and the USA, and who advised Eliot stylistically.[6] Pound's generosity was to be much later repaid by Eliot's campaign for his mentor, when Pound was being accused of treason and pushed into a lunatic asylum.

THE JEWISH PRESENCE

The presence of Jews in commerce and as a factor in undermining tradition did not go unnoticed in many quarters of both Left and Right during this time, including Social Credit and artistic circles. Hillaire Belloc, the Catholic social theorist and author, wrote a book on the subject in which he considered Jews as collectively "an alien body within society."[7] Ezra Pound got into much trouble eventually, and there continues to be a good deal of hand-wringing as to whether Eliot was an "anti-Semite" or, if he was, whether he remained so.[8]

Eliot's early poem, "Burbank with a Baedekker, Bleistein with a Cigar" (1919) examines the differences in mentality between two tourists in Venice, one tellingly named Bleistein, seeing

---

[6] T. Sharpe, *T. S. Eliot: A Literary Life* (New York: St. Martin's Press, 1991), p. 46.

[7] H. Belloc, *The Jews* (London: Butler & Tanner, 1937).

[8] A. D. Moody, *Thomas Stearns Eliot: Poet* (London: Cambridge University Press, 1980), pp. 370-71.

nothing but commerce. Bleistein is characterised stereotypically:

> But this or such was Bleistein's way:
> A saggy bending of the knees
> And elbows, with the palms turned out,
> Chicago Semite Viennese . . .
> On the Rialto once.
> The rats are underneath the piles.
> The jew is underneath the lot.
> Money in furs.
> The boatman smiles . . .

The following year Eliot evokes the stereotypical Jewish landlord in "Gerontion":

> Here I am, an old man in a dry month,
> Being read to by a boy, waiting for rain.
> I was neither at the hot gates
> Nor fought in the warm rain
> Nor knee deep in the salt marsh, heaving a cutlass,
> Bitten by flies, fought.
> My house is a decayed house,
> And the jew squats on the window sill, the owner,
> Spawned in some estaminet of Antwerp,
> Blistered in Brussels, patched and peeled in London.[9]

A Jewish character is also portrayed in less than flattering terms in "Sweeney Among the Nightingales":

> The silent vertebrate in brown
> Contracts and concentrates, withdraws;
> Rachel *née* Rabinovitch
> Tears at the grapes with murderous paws . . .[10]

The common theme that emerges in the Jewish characters of

---

[9] T. S. Eliot, *Poems* (New York: Alfred A Knopf, 1920), "Gerontion."
[10] Eliot, *Poems*, "Sweeney Among the Nightingales."

Eliot's verse is that of the cosmopolitan, vulgar Jew who epitomized "new wealth" and bought his way into high society, but was kept at arm's length by England's "old money," who saw wealthy Jews as having the thinnest veneer of cultivation. It is certainly why Eliot's characterization would not have been greeted with the outrage that it met in post-war years.

Over a decade later Eliot again alludes to Jewish influence in his lecture at the University of Virginia, advising that tradition can only develop where the population is homogeneous:

> Where two or more cultures exist in the same place they are likely to be fiercely self-conscious or both to become adulterate. What is still more important is unity of religious background; and reasons of race and religion combine to make any large numbers of free-thinking Jews undesirable. There must be a proper balance between urban and rural, industrial and agricultural development. And a spirit of excessive tolerance is to be deprecated.[11]

This passage concisely expresses all of Eliot's primary views on the matter of tradition, and is the antithesis of everything that is signified by the word *liberalism*. Yet because there is a reference to Jews, and in particular, because it was published when Hitler had just assumed power, it becomes particularly problematic to those who admire Eliot's work (or Pound's, or Hamsun's), but reach a crisis of morality when confronted with the writer's illiberality.[12] Professor Sharpe, for example, refers to "some extremely unlovely passages to do with Jews and Jewishness in Eliot's writing."[13]

Sharpe and others have pointed out that Eliot did not allow *After Strange Gods* to be reprinted in later years; nonetheless Eli-

---

[11] T. S. Eliot, *After Strange Gods: A Primer of Modern Heresy* (London: Faber and Faber, 1934), pp. 19–20. The full text can be read at: http://www.archive.org/stream/afterstrangegods00eliouoft/afterstrangegods00eliouoft_djvu.txt

[12] Moody, *Thomas Stearns Eliot: Poet*, pp. 370–71.

[13] Sharpe, *T. S. Eliot: A Literary Life*, p. 171.

ot's illiberality remained unredeemed, as indicated by his comment in 1961 that he saw nothing he would change for the reprinting of *Notes Towards a Definition of Culture*.[14] The refusal to allow *After Strange Gods* to be republished seems to have been primarily because Eliot did not like the polemical style, and he regretted his criticism of Pound and D. H. Lawrence. *The Catholic Herald* asks why Eliot did not withdraw "Burbank with a Baedekker, Bleistein with a Cigar," as he did *After Strange Gods*, if he had truly repented his previous convictions in the wake of the Holocaust:

> After the war Eliot prudently withdrew this book from circulation and never re-published it. So why did he not withdraw the equally damning poem "Burbank with a Baedeker: Bleistein with a Cigar" from his *Selected Poems*, published in 1948 . . . ? It was still included in my own copy of his *Collected Poems 1909–1962*, published in 1963 and which I read that same year. Was it an oversight or did the magnitude of the Holocaust not impinge on Eliot's consciousness?[15]

Why the Holocaust should be the criterion by which cultural critique is censored is yet, however, to be explained by any of these detractors other than in terms of a pervasive Western moral repentance that is as stifling to honest analysis as Lysenko's dogma was to Soviet biology.

"CLASSICIST, ROYALIST, ANGLO-CATHOLIC"

Eliot was primarily a Christian and a royalist. In Social Credit he saw the economic aspect of the Anglo-Catholic *via media*, or middle path between socialism and capitalism.[16] His aim was to

---

[14] T. S. Eliot, *Notes Towards A Definition of Culture*, "Preface to the 1962 Edition," p. 7.

[15] F. Philips, "The Poet Who Confronted T. S. Eliot Over his Anti-Semitism," *CatholicHerald.co.uk*, October 3, 2011, http://www.catholicherald.co.uk/commentandblogs/2011/10/03/the-poet-who-confronted-t-s-eliot-over-his-anti-semitism/

[16] A. S. Dale, *T. S. Eliot: The Philosopher Poet* (Lincoln, Nebraska:

revive religion as the foundation for a cultural, aesthetic outlook. A. S. Dale comments that Eliot "wanted to affect the reader as a whole human being, morally and aesthetically."[17] This was not something that secular-humanist society, whether as capitalism or as socialism, was inclined to do.

While other aesthetes were choosing Communism or fascism, shaping up as the two great antagonists for the control of the world, Eliot chose "Anglo-Catholicism." It was nonetheless a position on the Right, albeit critical of Hitler and Mussolini, but rejecting the Leftism of Bloomsbury.

Hence, when the intelligentsia was all aflutter over the Spanish Civil War in their near unanimous support for the Republican church-burners and nun-killers, in the interests of stopping Franco and Reaction, Eliot responded to a slanted survey on the issue circulated among the literati saying that he would remain neutral, itself a heresy in that milieu.[18]

Again, unlike others of the literati who joined Left or Right, Eliot did not propose a particular governmental system. However, he did believe that Christians should present their opinions on a solid Christian basis and form a community from which such ideals could emanate.[19] Hence, when Eliot published *Essays Ancient and Modern* and *Collected Poems 1909–1935*, he drew criticism for attempting to establish a "Christian poetics" and for discussing a "Christian polity."[20]

Eliot had converted to the Anglo-Catholic branch of the Church of England in 1927, and he remained an ardent worshipper until his death in 1966. His faith was the crucial element in his thinking and creativity. The most succinct self-description of his outlook was that of a "classicist in literature, royalist in politics, and Anglo-Catholic in religion."[21]

It was an echo of the statement made in 1913 by the seminal

Universe, 2004), p. 131.
[17] Dale, p. 129.
[18] Dale, p. 129.
[19] Dale, p. 132.
[20] Dale, p. 132.
[21] T. S. Eliot, *For Lancelot Andrewes*, 1928, "Preface."

French Rightist and Academician, Charles Maurras, leader of the militant Action Française, describing his "counter-revolutionary" beliefs as *"classique, catholique, monarchique,"*[22] that is to say, the antithesis of the Jacobin foundations of the French Republic. Indeed, Eliot was to state that "most of the concepts which might have attracted me in Fascism I seem already to have found, in a more digestible form, in the work of Charles Maurras. I say in a more digestible form, because I think they have a closer applicability in England than those of Fascism."[23]

Because Fascism treated monarchy as "a convenience," it was unacceptable to Eliot. Nevertheless, it was nonetheless preferable to Communism. His preference was for "the powerful king and the able minister," rather than the Fascist formula of "a powerful dictator and a nominal king." Although Maurras was accused of being a fascist and was to be tried as a collaborator after World War II,[24] he advocated tradition, not fascism, and was of much interest to Eliot as a leading classicist and intellectual and cultural exponent of the Right. Maurras believed, like Eliot, that monarchy and aristocracy would protect the humble from the "ambitious politician."[25]

Eliot's interest in Anglo-Catholicism was already inspired by his first visit to England in 1911, when he enthused about visiting Westminster Abbey and other great churches in London. Looking at their great architecture, Eliot saw the living embodiment of a past high culture epitomized by the architect of St. Paul's Cathedral, Sir Christopher Wren, a royalist commissioned by Charles II to rebuild fifty-one churches after the great fire of

---

[22] C. Maurras, *Nouvelle Revue Francaise*, March 1913, cited by B. Spurr, *Anglo-Catholic in Religion* (The Lutterworth Press, 2010), p. vii.

[23] T. S. Eliot, *The Criterion*, December 1928, p. 289, quoted by Alastair Hamilton, p. 275.

[24] Maurras, like many French Rightists, was anti-German, but a prominent supporter of the Vichy regime of Marshall Pétain. Maurras opposed collaboration with the German occupation but also opposed the Allies and regarded the Resistance as banditry. In 1945 Maurras was sentenced to life imprisonment and died in 1952.

[25] T. S. Eliot, "Mr. Barnes and Mr. Rowes," *The Criterion*, July 1929.

1666.[26] Here was the nexus of the pivotal elements of enduring culture: monarchy and faith, under which culture flourished in ways impossible under liberalism and equality.

Eliot, as an employee in the City, could not help contrast the churches that had been built by Wren in grand classical style, and in the tradition of the High Church, with the "hideous banks and commercial houses, the churches being the only redeeming quality of some vulgar street." He was writing at a time when there was a proposal to demolish nineteen of the churches.[27]

The proposal for the demolition of "redundant" churches in the City can readily be seen to symbolize the dichotomy of the modern world: the functionalism of commerce destroying the vestiges of high culture. In 1926, a year before Eliot's official conversion, he and literary scholar Bonamy Dobrée led a hymn-chanting protest through the streets of the City, which succeeded in saving the churches.[28]

However, Eliot believed in traditions that were locally rooted. This is why he opted to become an Anglo-Catholic, rather than a Roman Catholic, to which he would certainly have converted had he decided to reside in France rather than Britain. Becoming a British citizen and converting to the Church of England were part of the same process, as the religious tradition of a nation was the central ingredient of a national culture. However, churches were degraded by nationalism, and Eliot eschewed the concept of the Church of England as a "national Church." Rather, it is nationalism that should be predicated on faith, rather than faith serve as a tool of nationalism.[29] The Church of England was a national Church, but Eliot thought that it should be "the Catholic Church in England."[30] Anglo-Catholicism is that body within Anglicanism that maintains the Church of England is a branch of Catholicism rather than Protestantism.

---

[26] B. Spurr, *Anglo-Catholic in Religion*, p. 35.
[27] Spurr, p. 36.
[28] Spurr, p. 40.
[29] Spurr, p. 44.
[30] Spurr, p. 44.

CLASSICISM & ROMANTICISM

Founded by T. E. Hulme, English classicism was the other primary element in Eliot's doctrine. It was an aesthetic outlook that also had a major influence on Eliot's friends Ezra Pound, and Wyndham Lewis.

Although Eliot imbibed the classicism of Maurras and Hulme in France and Britain respectively, he had already become a classicist under the tutelage of Irving Babbitt at Harvard, who taught a course on "Literary Criticism in France." His was a nonconformist rejection of egalitarianism and industrialism, and a call for "standards" and "discipline"[31] against the orthodox American standard of economic "success" as the measure of all things.

Hence, when Eliot arrived in England he had already become a classicist and had rejected the triumphant doctrines of "progress," "liberty," and "equality." Eliot taught classicism contra romanticism in 1916 at Oxford University as an extension course of six lectures on modern French literature. The courses included a study of Rousseau's *Social Contract* and of the French classicist Maurras.[32] Rousseau, as the representative of Romanticism, was described by Eliot as involved in a struggle against "*authority* in matters of religion, *aristocracy* and *privilege* in government." His main doctrinal tendencies were "exaltation of the *personal* and *individual* above the *typical*, emphasis upon *feeling* rather than *thought*, humanitarianism: belief in the fundamental goodness of human nature, deprecation of *form* in art, and glorification of *spontaneity*." "His great faults were intense egotism," and "insincerity." Eliot wrote in the description of his course:

> Romanticism stands for *excess* in any direction. It splits up into two directions: escape from the world of fact, and devotion to brute fact. The two great currents of the 19th century — vague emotionality and the apotheosis of science

---

[31] Ackroyd, pp. 35–36.

[32] T. S. Eliot, "Syllabus of a Course of Six Lectures on modern French Literature by T Stearns Eliot," Oxford Extension Lectures, Oxford University, 1916.

(realism) alike spring from Rousseau.[33]

From Eliot's cogent description of the two common but antithetical tendencies that spring from Romanticism, we might understand how the French Revolution, proclaimed in the name of "Reason," assumed the most irrational forms. It erected substitute religions devoted to the "Goddess of Reason" and to the "Supreme Being," complete with hymns, liturgy, and holy days in the name of the Revolution.

The reaction against Romanticism started at the beginning of the 20th century in "a return to the ideals of classicism." Eliot explained the principles of classicism as *"form* and *restraint* in art, *discipline* and *authority* in religion, *centralization* in government (either as socialism or a monarchy). The classicist point of view has been defined as essentially a belief in Original Sin—the necessity of austere discipline."

Classicism obviously lends itself to doctrines of the Right, and Eliot refers to this when stating "a classicist in art and literature will be therefore likely to adhere to a monarchical form of government, and to the Catholic Church."

As for the reference to "socialism" being a manifestation of classicism along with monarchism, what Eliot meant can be discerned from his allusion to "syndicalism, more radical than 19th century socialism." This and monarchism "express revolt against the same state of affairs, and consequently tend to meet."

A classicist socialism had been emerging in France from the late 19th century, rejecting the Romanticist origins of the bourgeois Left and the Republic. Elements of the Right around Maurras, and of the Left, represented by the syndicalist Georges Sorel, were synthesizing a doctrine that included royalism and eschewed the old materialist interpretations of socialism. Eliot recognized the development of this movement, referring to "Neo-Catholicism" in France as partly a "political movement associated with monarchism, and partly a reaction against the sceptical scientific view of the 19th century. It is strongly marked in socialistic writers as well. It must not be confused with modern-

---

[33] "Syllabus."

ism, which is a purely intellectual movement."[34]

Lecture IV dealt with "Royalism and Socialism," where Eliot, explaining the emerging synthesis, stated that "contemporary socialism has much in common with royalism." Amongst those studied were Maurras and Sorel, the latter representing a "more violent reaction against bourgeois socialism."[35] This developed into fascism, especially from among the most militant adherents of Action Française, who were impatient with old methods.[36] However, Eliot as an Anglo-Catholic seeking the *via media* was to consider Social Credit as a sufficient mechanism for social change without recourse to the fascism that Ezra Pound mixed with Social Credit.

TRADITION & CULTURE

Eliot's primary focus was not political but *metapolitical*. He explained this after the Second World War in his lectures on the unity of European culture, which will be examined below. His writing, his contribution to the corpus of great European Literature, was his statement of rebellion against cultural pathology. He was writing consciously as a member of the European cultural stream:

> The historical sense compels a man to write not merely with his own generation in his bones, but with a feeling that the whole of the literature of Europe from Homer and within it the whole of the literature of his own country has a simultaneous existence and composes a simultaneous order.[37]

One sees the contrast with the Romantic who is rootless, an individualist of his moment, where nothing other than the Ego is of relevance, and there is no criterion upon which to determine

---

[34] "Syllabus."

[35] "Syllabus."

[36] Z. Sternhell, *Neither Left Nor Right: Fascist Ideology in France* (New Jersey: Princeton University Press, 1996).

[37] T. S. Eliot, *The Sacred Wood: Essays on Poetry & Criticism* (New York: Alfred A Knopf, 1921), "Tradition the Individual Talent," I: 3.

what is "art" and what is junk: cultural nihilism, marketable because there is an audience that is itself rootless.

The artist, then, is part of a tradition, unless art becomes detached and thereby debased, as it now generally is, based on market values and the discernment of art critics who are themselves detached from any tradition. For Eliot and most of the other artists who turned to the Right,[38] a flourishing culture meant not flux and continual "innovation" and "experimentation," which is now lauded as the epitome of artistic "free expression." Rather, it meant order, duration, and a connection with the past, present, and future. As Eliot pointed out, however, this did not mean stasis and the copying of earlier works. Again, it is the principle of *via media*. Of the importance of tradition to the artist Eliot wrote:

> No poet, no artist of any art, has his complete meaning alone. His significance, his appreciation is the appreciation of his relation to the dead poets and artists. You cannot value him alone; you must set him, for contrast and comparison, among the dead. I mean this as a principle of æsthetic, not merely historical, criticism. The necessity that he shall conform, that he shall cohere, is not one-sided; what happens when a new work of art is created is something that happens simultaneously to all the works of art which preceded it. The existing monuments form an ideal order among themselves, which is modified by the introduction of the new (the really new) work of art among them. The existing order is complete before the new work arrives; for order to persist after the supervention of novelty, the *whole* existing order must be, if ever so slightly, altered; and so the relations, proportions, values of each work of art toward the whole are readjusted; and this is conformity between the old and the new. Whoever has approved this idea of order, of the form of European, of English literature, will not find it preposterous that the past should be altered by the present as much as the pre-

---

[38] The Italian Futurists were an exception.

sent is directed by the past. And the poet who is aware of this will be aware of great difficulties and responsibilities.[39]

Tradition thereby establishes a criterion of what "art" is—a far cry from today when we are continually reminded that art is anything that "challenges," provokes a "reaction," or has a "message." Eliot wrote of this artistic criterion:

> In a peculiar sense he will be aware also that he must inevitably be judged by the standards of the past. I say judged, not amputated, by them; not judged to be as good as, or worse or better than, the dead; and certainly not judged by the canons of dead critics. It is a judgment, a comparison, in which two things are measured by each other. To conform merely would be for the new work not really to conform at all; it would not be new, and would therefore not be a work of art. And we do not quite say that the new is more valuable because it fits in; but its fitting in is a test of its value—a test, it is true, which can only be slowly and cautiously applied, for we are none of us infallible judges of conformity. We say: it appears to conform, and is perhaps individual, or it appears individual, and may conform; but we are hardly likely to find that it is one and not the other.[40]

In 1925, Eliot wrote "The Hollow Men," which describes the state of what can be called Modern Man, who has no attachment, no place in a living tradition. It was written at a time when Eliot had had a breakdown. In her essay and analysis of the poem Heather Van Aelst cogently writes:

> "The Hollow Men" is essentially a poem of emptiness, Eliot's exploration of the state of his own soul as one of many modern souls suffering the same affliction. It is an empti-

---

[39] "Tradition the Individual Talent," I: 4.
[40] "Tradition the Individual Talent," I: 5.

ness caused by the condition of the modern world, a modern world in which men live only for themselves, failing to choose between good and evil. The souls in the poem whose condition we are supposed to be horrified by are not those who have sinned the most, but those who have not chosen whether or not to sin. They exist in a state in-between, a state in which their failure to make a decision causes an utter lack of hope and joy or pain. The heroes of this poem are those who clearly see this state and recognize its true horror.[41]

It expresses a cultural malady that was of concern to those such as Eliot, Yeats, Campbell, Pound, *et al.* who sought a way out of the quagmire, making their art their protest, while simultaneously contributing significantly to a tradition that bypasses the culture of the marketplace.

"The Hollow Men" could as well apply to modern man as a new species, represented by the majority within all classes and stations of life:

> We are the hollow men
> We are the stuffed men
> Leaning together
> Headpiece filled with straw.
> Alas! Our dried voices, when
> We whisper together
> Are quiet and meaningless
> As wind in dry grass

There is not even drama in the death of Western civilization, no last hurrah as in Spengler's scenario where a resurgence of Tradition led by modern "Caesars" overcomes Money, or as in ancient days, where a vigorous barbarian tribe overwhelms the dominant civilization that has become senile. For our own civilization the question is posed by Eliot as to its ending:

---

[41] Heather Van Aelst "Conclusions," http://aduni.org/~heather/occs/honors/Conclusions.htm

This is the way the world ends
Not with a bang but a whimper.

THE CRITERION

If Western civilization was inexorably heading towards an undramatic, almost indiscernible whimpering dissolution, then at least Eliot was to provide both a warning and an alternative to decline and death. Among Eliot's most important efforts was the founding of *The Criterion*, which was published from 1922 to 1939. The intent was to offer a cultural critique of the barbarity of modernism and champion a revival of Christian European culture; to provide an outlet for new writers, and to connect with others across Europe. When Eliot founded *The Criterion*, his ideas having been well-established since his tutelage under Babbitt at Harvard, he promoted it as a Tory publication representing "reaction" and "revolution," in opposition to "suburban democracy."[42]

First and foremost a Christian traditionalist, Eliot did not see the advent of Fascist Italy as optimistically as did Ezra Pound, although he refused to engage in intellectual tub-thumping, even when the treatment of Jews in National Socialist Germany was provoking widespread criticism. He described the prevailing anti-fascism as an "emotional outlet" for liberals, and as distracting them "from the true evils of their own society."[43] As mentioned earlier, he refused to take a position on the Spanish Civil War,[44] and even criticized Oxford when the University declined to participate in the bicentennial celebrations of the University of Göttingen in 1937, in protest against the restrictions against Jews. Eliot's position was that public institutions should not be political pawns, and that the associations of academics between nations should not be affected.

However, Eliot wondered whether Mussolini did represent "Authority and Tradition," in the historical European sense.[45]

---

[42] Ackroyd, p. 143.
[43] T. S. Eliot, *The Criterion*, Vol. 18, No. 70, October 1938, pp. 38–39.
[44] T. S. Eliot, *The Criterion*, Vol. 16, No. 63, January 1937, p. 290.
[45] T. S. Eliot, *The Criterion*, Vol. 4, No. 2, April 1926, p. 222.

He considered it likely that fascism was, like Communism, a substitute religion, and probably incompatible with Catholicism. For Eliot, the monarch and not the dictator symbolized the necessary authority, and this was tempered by the subjection of the throne to "one higher authority . . . the Church."[46] His was basically a neo-Medieval outlook.

In 1928, Eliot came to the defense of Maurras who, as leader of the L'Action Française, had been condemned by the Vatican.[47] Nearly a decade later he came to the defense of Wyndham Lewis, who did not disguise his sympathies for Fascism or his contempt for the Bloomsbury coterie, Eliot stating that "anyone who is not enthusiastic about the fruits of liberalism must be unpopular with the Anglo-Saxon majority."[48] Even in 1960, Eliot insisted that the word "fascist" is "flung by *massenmensch* at some, who like Lewis, choose to walk alone." [49]

In the June 1928 issue of *The Criterion* Eliot clarified his position, stating that the problems with civilization would be studied. He included in that issue a review of *Wealth, Virtual Wealth and Debt*, by the economic reformer Professor Frederick Soddy,[50] whose book was a seminal influence on the thinking of the early banking reformers. The review of the Soddy book (by J. McAlpine) explained that the medieval era had a social order based on the Church, which was organized through guilds, in which "money-dealing," was condemned, and in which faith was interwoven through the social fabric. The remnants of this traditional order were finally destroyed with the Industrial Revolution and domination by "a cash relationship." Clearly, Eliot held the same outlook, which was also the outlook of Orage whose influence promoted the careers of many new talents, including

---

[46] T. S. Eliot, *The Criterion*, Vol. 13, No. 53, July 1934, pp. 628–30.

[47] M. R. Stevens, "T. S. Eliot's Neo-Medieval Economics," *Journal of Markets & Morality*, Vol. 2, No. 2, Fall 1999, p. 235.

[48] T. S. Eliot, Review of Wyndham Lewis' *The Lion and the Fox* (1927) in *Twentieth Century Verse*, No. 6/7, November/December 1937, pp. 6–9.

[49] T. S. Eliot, "Foreword," Wyndham Lewis, 1933, *One-Way Song* (London: Methuen, 1960), p. 10.

[50] Stevens, p. 236.

Eliot and Pound.

In keeping with this "neo-medievalism," Eliot sought a return to a rural society, harking back to the organic society that had existed prior to industrialism and urbanization. Hence, in October 1931 Eliot wrote in *The Criterion* that agriculture ought to be "saved" because it is "the foundation for the good life in society; it is, in fact, the normal life."

For Eliot, economics and politics must be subjected first to moral and spiritual foundations. From these foundations economic and political problems are resolved. Writing in 1933, Eliot disputes the notion that political and economic reform must arrive first, followed by the moral question. A new economic system must be related to "a moral system." "Moralists and philosophers must supply the foundations of statesmanship, though they never appear in the forum."[51] This also alludes to the purpose of *The Criterion*, in forming a metapolitical school of moralists and philosophers who could reshape the social and moral order (and consequently the political and economic order), not just of Britain, but of Europe, whose culture Eliot regarded as unitary.

Articles on Social Credit published during 1935 dealt specifically with the economic question. *The Criterion* of July 1935 carried reviews by well-known commentator on economics, R. McNair Wilson, dealing with six books about Social Credit. Wilson stated that European civilization came into being on the basis of an economic system that repudiated usury, giving rise to the flowering of medieval culture, when, with an abundance of leisure (100 holy days plus the 52 Sundays) "small villages" were able to build magnificent cathedrals which endure to the present. Indeed, it is a fundamental principle of Social Credit that its system of economics would again provide an abundance both of general prosperity and of leisure, enabling culture to flourish again. What eventuated in the modern world has not been increased leisure and wider prosperity, despite the prospects held out by mechanization. Rather, there has been an *increase* in both working hours and in the retirement age. The same

---

[51] T. S. Eliot, "Commentary," *The Criterion*, July 1933.

problems have only been exacerbated in the present day.

The final issue of *The Criterion* carried these parting words from Eliot, in summation of his outlook: "For myself, a right political philosophy came more and more to imply a right theology—and right economics to depend upon right ethics: leading to emphases which somewhat stretched the original framework of a literary review."[52] This was the predicament of Pound, Yeats, Lawrence, Campbell, and all the other literati who saw culture as endangered by mass society engendered alike by Bolshevism, capitalism, and democracy. Men such as Pound saw the answer in a counter-modern doctrine, Fascism; while most, like Eliot, Yeats, and Campbell saw the answer in reaction and looked on Fascism suspiciously as yet another revolt of the masses.

AFTER STRANGE GODS

Industrialism and the concomitant phenomena of cosmopolitanism and alien immigration undermine the tradition upon which culture is based by breaking the chain which transmits culture through generations. In a lecture at the University of Virginia in 1933 (published the following year as *After Strange Gods: A Primer of Modern Heresy*), Eliot stated that the USA had not, and probably would not, recover from the Civil War, which was a victory of plutocracy and industrialism against tradition and agrarianism. He said to his Virginia audience that "the chances for the re-establishment of a native culture are perhaps better here than in New England. You are farther away from New York; you have been less industrialized and less invaded by foreign races; and you have a more opulent soil."[53]

The reference to New York can be seen as an allusion to the negative impact of cosmopolitanism on culture. Eliot proceeded to comment that the destruction of the soil also brought the destruction of the native qualities of a people, given that there is a two-way influence between race and soil. He referred to his native New England as "the half-dead mill towns of southern New

---

[52] T. S. Eliot, "Last Words," *The Criterion*, January 1939.

[53] T. S. Eliot, *After Strange Gods: A Primer of Modern Heresy* (London: Faber and Faber, 1934), p. 16.

Hampshire and Massachusetts":

> It is not necessarily those lands which are the most fertile or most favoured in climate that seem to me the happiest, but those in which a long struggle of adaptation between man and his environment has brought out the best qualities of both; in which the landscape has been moulded by numerous generations of one race, and in which the landscape in turn has modified the race to its own character.[54]

Eliot commended those who wished for a revived agrarian South who, despite being ridiculed as nurturing an impossible dream, were nonetheless embarking on a worthy cause against "the whole current of economic determinism," "a god before whom we fall down and worship with all kinds of music." However, Eliot stated:

> I believe that these matters may ultimately be determined by what people want; that when anything is generally accepted as desirable, economic laws can be upset in order to achieve it; that it does not so much matter at present whether any measures put forward are practical, as whether the aim is a good aim, and the alternatives intolerable. There are, at the present stage, more serious difficulties in the revival or establishment of a tradition and a way of life, which require immediate consideration.[55]

In conflict with economic determinism, "What I mean by tradition involves all those habitual actions, habits, and customs, from the most significant religious rite to our conventional way of greeting a stranger, which represent the blood kinship of the same people living in the same place."[56]

This conception of tradition repudiates the notion of multiculturalism, which is a manifestation of economic determinism,

---

[54] *After Strange Gods*, p. 17.
[55] *After Strange Gods*.
[56] *After Strange Gods*, p. 18.

whether in its capitalistic or socialistic forms. Eliot stated that where more than one culture exists in a locality the formation and transmission of a culture is subverted. Eliot was not advocating racial supremacy, which he viewed as clinging "to traditions as a way of asserting our superiority over less favoured peoples." What is required for a tradition to become established is a sense of place and permanence. "The population should be homogeneous; where two or more cultures exist in the same place they are likely either to be fiercely self-conscious or both to become adulterate."[57]

Eliot's recommendation has, of course, become ever more impossible, as capitalism has developed until we have what is today called "globalization." There are no settled or homogenous communities, and a new form of economic nomadism has formed a cosmopolitan class devoid of any attachments to locality, custom or tradition. This condition has been lauded by G. Pascal Zachary in *The Global Me* as virtually a new human species at the service of global capitalism[58]

Against what is today championed by men like Zachary as the unlimited possibilities of economic advance offered by the global village and the global market place, Eliot contends: "We must also remember that in spite of every means of transport that can be devised the local community must always be the most permanent." This concept of the local community for Eliot even took precedence over the nation, which was only useful insofar as it allowed for the stability of the community, which in turn was a grouping of families, rooted to place through generations. A nation's "strength and its geographical size depend upon the comprehensiveness of a way of life which can harmonise parts with distinct local characters of their own."[59] Hence, regionalism, or separatism, will arise when the nation-state becomes centralized and intrudes upon local tradition, for

---

[57] *After Strange Gods*, p. 19.

[58] G. Pascal Zachary, *The Global Me: Why Nations Will Succeed or Fail in the Next Generation* (New South Wales: Australia, Allen and Unwin, 2000).

[59] *After Strange Gods*, p. 20.

"It is only a law of nature, that local patriotism, when it represents a distinct tradition and culture, takes precedence over a more abstract national patriotism."[60]

For those who interpret the Right as synonymous with nationalism and loyalty to the nation-state, this repudiation of nationalistic and statist sanctity will appear confusing. However, the Right is a manifestation of tradition rather than of nation-states, which destroyed the traditional principalities, regions, and city-states that comprised the high culture of Western civilization. Eliot points out that "the consciousness of 'the nation' as the social unit is a very recent and contingent experience. It belongs to a limited historical period and is bound up with certain specific happenings."[61] Rather, "genuine patriotism" only has depth when there is a society "in which people have local attachments to their small domain and small community, and remain, generation after generation, in the same place." [62]

This is a call to reject cosmopolitanism, universalism, and urbanization: all the symptoms of the modern epoch of decay, and to return to the land, to the village, to the produce markets and church; all that which seems evoked by the word *parish*. One is reminded of the nostalgia for the organic society, stable and transmitting a fixed culture generation after generation, evoked by Knut Hamsun in such novels as *Growth of the Soil*.

THE IDEA OF A CHRISTIAN SOCIETY

The Criterion ceased publication as the Second World War approached. Eliot saw the rise of fascism and of nationalistic impulses as a disappearance of the "European Mind," which he had sought to revivify. Fascism and nationalism represent variants of modernity, and indeed spring from the same Enlightenment milieu as rationalism and liberalism, despite the traditionalism found in most varieties of fascism.

Not unlike Eliot, reactionaries such as Yeats and Julius Evola

---

[60] *After Strange Gods*, p. 20.
[61] *After Strange Gods*, p. 20. Eliot is here quoting V. A. Demant, *God, Man and Society*, p. 146.
[62] T. S. Eliot, "Commentary," *The Criterion*, Vol. 11, October 1931.

rejected fascism and statist nationalism for the same reasons: they represented mass mobilization; they were plebeian and modern; they were championed by Futurists under Marinetti in Italy, rejecting all tradition; they were intrinsically republican and centralist.

On the other hand, Eliot, as a reactionary in the most positive sense of the word, was a royalist and decentralist. He looked to a Europe of faith, to the gentry and the nobility, rather than the bureaucrat and the technocrat. He preferred farm, cottage, and church to steel and mechanization. Eliot's Europe, like that of Yeats and others, was dealt the death blow by the Second World War, as it had been dealt an earlier, almost lethal blow by the First World War, from which it had been nowhere near recovery.

Eliot even expressed his reservations about fascism in a now little-known play that was performed at Saddlers Wells Theatre, London, which depicted with equal disquiet contending Redshirts and Blackshirts. Nevertheless, it should not be thought that Eliot had become some sort of liberal who had repudiated earlier views under the pressure of anti-fascist conformity, a position that some have well-meaningly attempted in Eliot's defense against attacks from Leftist critics.[63]

Eliot's answer was, as ever, a return to Christianity as the social ethos. Eliot expounded this view in *The Idea of a Christian Society*, a work published shortly after the demise of *The Criterion*, in 1939. A society founded on the Christian ethos would "compel changes in our organization of industry and commerce and financial credit," and it would facilitate rather than (as it does at present) impede a life of devotion for those capable of it.[64]

On the eve of war with the totalitarian states, Eliot did not shrink from castigating the nebulousness of the political terms that had assumed sanctity in the Western world: "liberalism"

---

[63] G. Simmers, "T. S. Eliot's Attack on Anti-Semitism," http://greatwarfiction.wordpress.com/tseliots-attack-on-anti-semitism/

[64] T. S. Eliot, *The Idea of a Christian Society* (London: Faber and Faber, 1939), p. 11.

and "democracy." In particular, "democracy" has attained the height of popularity, and even those who sympathized with the Hitler regime used the word in a positive sense, while legitimately claiming (in agreement with Eliot) that what governs the "democratic" states is "financial oligarchy." The doctrine that continued to animate democracy is "liberalism," and here Eliot maintained his critical attitude, stating that liberalism "still permeates our minds and affects our attitude towards much of life . . . [and] tends to release energy rather than to accumulate it, to relax, rather than to fortify."

> It is a movement not so much defined by its end, as by its starting point; away from, rather than towards, something definite; and the destination is likely to present a very different picture when arrived at, from the vaguer image formed in imagination. By destroying traditional social habits of the people, by dissolving their natural collective consciousness into individual constituents, by licensing the opinions of the most foolish, by substituting instruction for education, by encouraging cleverness rather than wisdom, the upstart rather than the qualified, by fostering a notion of *getting on* to which the alternative is a hopeless apathy, liberalism can prepare the way for that which is its own negation: the artificial, mechanized or brutalized control, which is a desperate remedy for its chaos. [65]

It is here that the fascist can justly interject that "Liberalism is the handmaiden of Bolshevism," but the reactionary can also point out that liberalism paved the way for both capitalism, with its focus on property relations enshrined as sacrosanct in the French Revolutionary Declaration of the Rights of Man and the Citizen and the American Revolutionary Bill of Rights, and even fascism which arose from the concepts of the nation-state against thrones and altars, of the Revolutions of 1776 and 1789, and those of Europe in 1848.

The most acute forms of liberal dissolution are in states that

---

[65] *The Idea of a Christian Society,* pp. 16–17.

have become most industrialized. Hence, men and women of all classes are "detached from tradition, alienated from religion, and susceptible to mass suggestion: in other words, a mob. And a mob will be no less a mob if it is well fed, well clothed, well housed, and well disciplined."[66] Here we see cogently expressed the concerns that took some of Eliot's contemporaries (Pound, Lawrence, Yeats, *et al.*) to the Right. The rise of the mob was concomitant with that of liberalism and democracy, and such a society was not conducive to high culture, but rather to barbarity. Today it seems superfluous to make any comment on the accuracy of the predictions of Eliot and company on the results of liberalism on the social and cultural body.

The alternative to the dissolutive impact of liberalism is the basic social unit that Eliot identified in England as the parish, a "unitary community" of a "religious-social" character, which has been undermined by industrialism and urbanization.[67] The parish is:

> a small and mostly self-contained group attached to the soil and having its interests centred in a particular place, with a kind of unity which may be designed, but which also has to grow through generations. It is the idea, or ideal, of a community small enough to consist of a nexus of direct personal relationships, in which all iniquities and turpitudes will take the simple and easily appreciable form of wrong relations between one persona and another.[68]

A Christian society would be based on what would be habit and custom rather than law.[69] Alienation from the land caused by the Industrial Revolution, which started in England and then infected the entirety of Western civilization, led to urban drift and both to what Marx referred to as "the proletarianization of the yeomanry," and to the creation of the mercantile class in

---

[66] *The Idea of a Christian Society*, p. 21.
[67] *The Idea of a Christian Society*, p. 30.
[68] *The Idea of a Christian Society*, p. 31.
[69] *The Idea of a Christian Society*, p. 34.

place of the gentry. Eliot saw urbanization as ruinous to culture, as did contemporaries such as New Zealand poet Fairburn, Norwegian writer Hamsun, and English writer Henry Williamson. Eliot returned to the question of the rural basis of culture and demographic health, and the ruinous character of urbanization in *The Criterion* several years after discussing the problem in his Virginia address:

> To understand thoroughly what is wrong with agriculture is to understand what is wrong with nearly everything else: with the domination of Finance, with our ideals and system of Education, indeed with our whole philosophy of life. . . . What is fundamentally wrong is the *urbanization of mind* of which I have previously spoken, and which is increasingly prevalent as those who rule, those who speak, those who write, and developed in increasing numbers from an urban background. To have the right frame of mind . . . it is necessary that the greater part of the population, of all classes (so long as we have classes) should be settled in the country and be dependent upon it. One sees no hope whether in the Labour Party or in the equally unimaginative dominant section of the Conservative Party. There seems no hope in contemporary politics at all.[70]

Again, Eliot is looking to a bygone age, and toward the medieval, where the social organism was cohesive, society was predominantly rural, vocations were organized into guilds, and not only was there no "domination of Finance," usury was sin.

POST-WAR YEARS

Since Eliot had never endorsed fascism his support for Britain against the Axis during the Second World War was consistent with his view prior to the war, rather than a matter of conformity. However, Eliot saw the war as having ruined the unity of European culture, with a world now dominated by the USSR and

---

[70] T. S. Eliot, "A Commentary," *Criterion*, No. 18, Oct. 1938, pp. 59–60.

the USA.⁷¹

Eliot was not blinded by American blandishments. He disliked Roosevelt and held the USA accountable for both the Yalta accord, which delivered half of Europe to the USSR, and for the disintegration of the British Empire, which was one of several factors leading to what Eliot regarded as an impending Dark Age.⁷²

In 1947 Eliot's first wife Vivien died, and he was in declining health. He went to the US that year and also continued with religious retreats and observances. In 1948 he was awarded the Order of Merit.⁷³ That year he returned to America, where he continued writing a new play, *The One-Eyed Riley*, having been granted a visiting fellowship with Princeton University's Institute for Advanced Study. This was interrupted when he was awarded the Nobel Prize in Literature, which required attending the Stockholm ceremony. Also that year, the first of three volumes were published in his honor, *T. S. Eliot: A Symposium*.⁷⁴ *Notes Towards a Definition of Culture* was also published in 1948.⁷⁵

Eliot had not been compromised by the mania for liberalism, internationalism, and egalitarianism in the aftermath of the war. Writing in 1961 for a new edition of *Notes Towards a Definition of Culture* published in 1962, he stated that, on re-reading the book, he found nothing to retract.⁷⁶ His conception of society continued to be of classes as purveyors of the cultural legacy from generation to generation, rather than specialized "elites" confined to limited functions. This class-based culture was not, however, the property of a single class but of the social organism as a totality, the health and continuation of a culture being reliant "on the health of the culture of the people."⁷⁷ The whole of

---

⁷¹ A. S. Dale, *T. S. Eliot: The Philosopher Poet* (Lincoln, Nebraska: iUniverse, 2004), p. 161.

⁷² Dale, p. 162

⁷³ Dale, p. 168.

⁷⁴ Dale, p. 169.

⁷⁵ Dale, p. 170.

⁷⁶ Eliot, *Notes Towards a Definition of Culture* (London: Faber & Faber, 1962), p. 7.

⁷⁷ *Notes Towards a Definition of Culture*, p. 35.

the population should be active in cultural activities, albeit "not all in the same activities or on the same level," but on the basis of what he called "group culture."[78] The social order should allow for the best—whether in politics or the arts—to "rise to the top" and influence taste.[79] Eliot did not view the elimination of class, including the "upper class" in the name of equality, as something desirable. While it might have little effect in a state of lower development, elsewhere, it can be "a disaster."[80] The danger of elites replacing classes is that such elites have no common bond other than as what we might call professional functionaries who, states Eliot, lack "social continuity." A class-structured society, on the other hand, is a "natural society." Therefore, Eliot championed the aristocracy but not an "aristocratic society" *per se*. The difference is that Eliot's vision was of a cohesive social structure in which aristocracy played its role, which was as essential and valuable as all the others.[81] This we might identify as an *organic society*: a social organism based on "a continuous gradation of cultural levels" in which the "upper levels" are distinguished as possessing the highest degrees of cultural consciousness. Each class would have different responsibilities suited to it, rather than the egalitarianism of democracy that becomes "oppressive for the conscientious and licentious for the rest." The social organism is founded on family, which is the means by which culture is transmitted over generations.[82] I suggest that the way of looking at how such a society worked was via the guilds of medieval Europe, and we might recall here that Eliot had started his vocation as a close associate of Orage, a prominent advocate for both Social Credit and guild socialism, and that Eliot opened the pages of *The Criterion* with such views.

However, in the aftermath of the Second World War, with the advent of a Labour Government in Britain, and the domination of the US over Europe, Eliot's focus for change moved from Brit-

---

[78] *Notes Towards a Definition of Culture*, pp. 38–39.
[79] *Notes Towards a Definition of Culture*, p. 45.
[80] *Notes Towards a Definition of Culture*, p. 46.
[81] *Notes Towards a Definition of Culture*, p. 48.
[82] *Notes Towards a Definition of Culture*, p. 48.

ain to the Continent, and to the survival of European civilization as a whole. In 1945 he expressed concern that what lay ahead was "centuries of barbarism" ushered in by the supremacy of technology.[83]

In 1946 he gave three radio talks to a German audience, which were reprinted as an appendix to *Notes*, entitled "The Unity of European Culture." He began by lauding the English language as the best specifically for writing poetry, but also as a language that itself represented the unity of European culture, in synthesizing German (Saxon), Scandinavian (Danish), French (Norman), Latin, and Celtic. Most importantly to the poet, each contributed its own "Rhythms," a composite of so many different European sources."[84] Of the fundamental unity among Europeans, "no one nation, no one language, would have achieved what it has, if the same art had not been cultivated in neighboring countries and in different languages. We cannot understand any one European literature without knowing a good deal about the others." European poetry is "a tissue of influences woven to and fro." Those poets who only knew their own tongue were nonetheless subject to influences from wider sources. The vitality of poetry must be maintained by a continual interaction from outside, while also having sources that are "peculiarly its own."[85]

While there had in recent times been an influence from Oriental sources, and Eliot did not advocate cultural isolation, he nonetheless stated that it is a shared history that provides the basis for a unitary cultural organism where "countries which share the most history, are the most important to each other, with respect to their future literature," as well as for the other arts. "Wherever a Virgil, a Dante, a Shakespeare, a Goethe is born, the whole future of European poetry is altered. . . . Every great poet adds something to the complex material out of which a future poetry will be written."[86] Hence, a tradition is accumu-

---

[83] Eliot, *Horizon*, August 1945.
[84] *Notes Towards a Definition of Culture*, p. 111.
[85] *Notes Towards a Definition of Culture*, pp. 112–13.
[86] *Notes Towards a Definition of Culture*, p. 114.

lated and transmitted, and forms the foundation for the future.

With *The Criterion*, Eliot had aimed for an interchange of new ideas across Europe, and this had been proceeding through contact with similar journals in France, Germany, Spain, and Italy. What emerged however, because of the political situation and the rise of national antagonisms before the war, was a cultural isolation among Europeans, which had a "numbing effect upon creativity" in each nation.[87] Eliot saw politics as divisive for culture.[88] Hence, we might understand why he chose to remain "neutral" on issues that preoccupied the intelligentsia, such as the Spanish Civil War. What *The Criterion* had sought, above political and national differences, was "an international fraternity of men of letters, within Europe, a bond which did not replace, but was perfectly compatible with, national loyalties, religious loyalties, and differences in political philosophy."[89]

Eliot viewed with concern political nationalism that denigrated other European cultures. But for the post-war world there emerged the problem of "the ideal of a world state in which there will, in the end, be only one universal world culture." Culture was an organism that had to grow and be nurtured like other living organisms, and could not be contrived through the machinery of government, including world government. The cultural health of Europe required that the culture of each country should remain unique, and that each should realize their relationship to the other on the basis of a "common element," "an interrelated history of thought and feeling and behaviour."[90]

Eliot sought to define culture to delineate the "material organisation of Europe" and the "spiritual organism of Europe." "If the latter dies, then what you organise will not be Europe, but merely a mass of human being speaking several different languages." One thinks immediately here of the artificial construct of the EEC.

Under such contrivances, even differences in language will

---

[87] *Notes Towards a Definition of Culture*, p. 116.
[88] *Notes Towards a Definition of Culture*, p. 117.
[89] *Notes Towards a Definition of Culture*, p. 118.
[90] *Notes Towards a Definition of Culture*, pp. 118–19.

no longer matter, since there will no longer be anything left to say that cannot be said in any other language. Further, there is a differentiation of "higher" and "lower" cultures, "higher" being "distinguished by differentiation in function," with a "less cultured and more cultured strata of society." While the culture of a laborer, a poet, a politician, a painter will all be different, "in a healthy society these are all parts of the same culture," and all these classes "will have a culture in common, which they do not share with other people of the same occupations in other countries." [91]

Hence Eliot's conception of society and culture was organic and repudiates not only cosmopolitism of all types, but notions of class struggle and economic determinism.

As always, the ultimate unitary factor for European culture remained, for Eliot, the Christian faith. "If Asia were converted to Christianity tomorrow, it would not thereby become a part of Europe." Christianity has shaped the arts and laws of Europe. The individual, although not personally confessing Christianity, will nonetheless have been shaped by that heritage.[92]

This organic, cultural unity is of a different character to that of the political loyalty demanded by statist ideologies. Here we have a reason why Eliot could not support fascism. It is also why he risked condemnation as being "pro-Nazi" for refusing to support Oxford's boycott of Göttingen University's bicentennial celebrations on political grounds: "No university ought to be merely a national institution, even if it is supported by the nation. The universities of Europe should have their common ideals, they should have their obligations towards each other."[93] They should serve cultural, not political ends, to preserve learning, pursue truth, and attain wisdom, rather than existing to fill a state's bureaucracy.

Eliot feared for the future of European culture, and the advance of barbarism via the primacy of technology. He appealed to "the men of letters of Europe" to transcend differences and

---

[91] *Notes Towards a Definition of Culture*, p. 120.
[92] *Notes Towards a Definition of Culture*, p. 122.
[93] *Notes Towards a Definition of Culture*, p. 123.

preserve and transmit the common cultural legacy "uncontaminated by political influences." He regarded the "spiritual possessions" of several thousand years as in "imminent peril."[94]

His warnings were prescient. The nightmare of soulnessness was unleashed and has grown exponentially under the impress of globalization. It is superfluous to comment in detail; it is evident on a daily basis to anyone attuned to the rhythms of history. When one academic can nonetheless still state in a biography of Eliot that "the barbarians did not arrive in his lifetime,"[95] that blindness is itself symptomatic of a cultural malaise.

One of Eliot's great post-war feats was his leading role in securing the release of Ezra Pound from St. Elizabeth's lunatic asylum in 1958, "largely as the result of Eliot's collaboration with Robert Frost and Archibald McLeish in petitioning the American government."[96]

Unlike Ezra Pound, during his lifetime Eliot seems to have mostly escaped the opprobrium illiberality attracts. However, after death he has become a figure of hatred, and in 1988 *The London Jewish Chronicle* condemned Jews who were involved in the T. S. Eliot Centenary Fund at the London Library.[97] Such meanness of spirit would not have biased Eliot's attitude towards others, including Jews, when considering the merits or otherwise of one's creativity; any more than it did the supposedly rabid "anti-Semite" Ezra Pound.

What the liberal critic is incapable of conceiving is that a cultural luminary such as Eliot, Hilaire Belloc, or Pound could — like the Zionist — be conscious of the otherness of the Jew in the Gentile society, while not necessarily harboring antagonism towards Jews on a personal basis. One such example is Eliot's letter of December 9, 1920 to Ezra Pound referring to the poetry of Louis Zukofsy as "highly intelligent and honourably Jewish."[98]

---

[94] *Notes Towards a Definition of Culture*, p. 124.
[95] Ackroyd, p. 273.
[96] Ackroyd, p. 329.
[97] M. Kakutani, "Critic's Notebook; Examining T. S. Eliot and Anti-Semitism: How Bad Was It?" *The New York Times*, August 22, 1989.
[98] Sharpe, *T. S. Eliot: A Literary Life*, p. 171.

For those concerned with the malaise of Western culture, the great contribution of Eliot was to *define* culture, and to establish, to use his own word, a *criterion* for art. It is a counterblast against those—the majority among today's artists, art critics, patrons, publishers, gallery owners, curators, etc.—who toss about clichés claiming that art is too "subjective," too personal to be defined; that there is no criterion, no standard, that art can be "anything." He also showed that tradition is not synonymous with stagnation and does not preclude innovation. Indeed Eliot, Ezra Pound, and others of that milieu were the great innovators of their time.

Counter-Currents/*North American New Right*
September 25 & 26, 2012

Chapter 4

P. R. STEPHENSEN

Percy Reginald "Inky" Stephensen (1901–1965) was one of Australia's pre-eminent "men of letters"—or "Australia's wild man of letters" as one biographer called him.[1] He also served as a ghostwriter of many books and as a mentor to aspiring writers. Like his New Zealand contemporary A. R. D. Fairburn, Stephensen sought to develop a distinct national culture for his homeland. His work as a publisher and political activist was dedicated to fostering this sense of "Australianity." Like many others of the Right, such as Ezra Pound, Roy Campbell, and Knut Hamsun, Stephensen has seldom been acknowledged, despite his pivotal role in developing an Australian literature and defining an Australian culture.[2]

Born in Queensland in 1901 of Scandinavian descent, Stephensen had a polemical disposition from an early age and was inclined towards the Left as a university student. In 1921, he was a founding member of the Australian Communist Party.[3] After graduating in the arts he took a teaching position in 1922 and formed a Communist association.[4] He was also one of the first to write an in-depth review of D. H. Lawrence's novel *Kangaroo*, while serving as a writer for a Labour Party newspaper in Brisbane, *The Daily Standard*. Several years later in England he became Lawrence's publisher.[5] In 1924 he was selected

---

[1] Craig Munro, *Inky Stephensen: Wild Man of Letters* (Brisbane: University of Queensland Press, 1992).

[2] Bruce Muirden remarks that, "Miles Franklin has noted, with justice, that Stephensen's key critical work, *The Foundations of Culture in Australia*, is 'more assiduously consulted than acknowledged.'" Muirden, *The Puzzled Patriots: The Story of the Australia First Movement* (Melbourne: Melbourne University Press, 1968), pp. 15–16.

[3] *The Puzzled Patriots*, p. 17.
[4] *The Puzzled Patriots*, p. 17.
[5] *The Puzzled Patriots*, p. 17.

as Queensland's Rhodes Scholar and enrolled in the School of Philosophy and Political Economics at Oxford.[6] He was one of the few members of the Communist Party at Oxford and was active in spreading propaganda in support of Indian independence.[7] Despite qualifying for his Bachelor's Degree in 1927 he never bothered collecting it. An Australian nationalist only obtained documentation of his studies in 2000.[8]

NIETZSCHE & BAKUNIN

Whatever Stephensen's ideological commitment to Communism, it seems likely that his motivation was a reaction against bourgeois society. As the publisher of the *London Aphrodite* during the late 1920s, Stephensen wrote an article in praise of the Russian anarchist Bakunin with particular attention to him as a man of pure action and vitality.[9] Stephensen's admiration was based on his view of Bakunin as a Nietzschean-style figure.[10] Stephensen describes Bakunin as what Nietzsche would have termed a "Higher Man," as forerunner of the "Over-Man,"[11] although it is doubtful whether Nietzsche himself would have applauded Bakunin's anarchism[12]: "Only one man has lived dangerously—Michael Bakunin. While Nietzsche postulated the Fore-runner, here was a fore-runner in deed," wrote Stephensen.

---

[6] *The Puzzled Patriots*, p. 17.

[7] *The Puzzled Patriots*, pp. 17–18.

[8] http://home.alphalink.com.au/~radnat/stephensen/prsdegree01.jpg

[9] P. R. Stephensen, "Bakunin," ca. 1928.

[10] Stephensen translated and published Nietzsche's *The Antichrist* in 1929.

[11] Friedrich Nietzsche, *Thus Spoke Zarathustra* (Harmondsworth: Penguin Books, 1969), "Of Higher Man," pp. 296-306.

[12] Nietzsche would not have applauded the revolutionary mob under any circumstance, although it is easy to see what Stephensen could perceive in Bakunin in Nietzschean terms, and the revolutionary desire to destroy the bourgeois order: "For today the petty people have become lord and master: they all preach submission and acquiescence and prudence and diligence and consideration and the long *et cetera* of petty virtues" (*Thus Spoke Zarathustra*, p. 298).

Stephensen contrasted the character of Bakunin as a revolutionary colossus astride the world against the archetypical English liberal "statesman" and his credo:

> This man, Bakunin, walked on the edge of precipices, and is a hero. I have little difficulty in preferring his character to that of, say, the much-esteemed Mr. Stanley Baldwin, whose inane posture of "Safety First" has actually been employed as a sedative to voters in the recent dull Elections in Britain. The Bakunin-principle of action was always "Safety-Last." Bakunin is essentially revolutionary, the antithesis of Baldwin. His type is surely not extinct. It must re-emerge, stronger, or the world dies.[13]

When Stephensen apocalyptically stated that the "world dies" unless the "Bakunin-principle" re-emerges, he already saw forewarnings of the age of "Machinery and its accompanying sacrifice to profit-scrambling." The First World War was a manifestation of this, which "has developed the Robot and crushed the man. We shall need the Bakunin-principle yet again."[14] He believed that any revolutionary theory that does not lead to street fighting is "fake, tepid air, not even hot."[15]

Like Bakunin, Stephensen at this time saw the need for destruction. Further, it was not "anarchism" *per se* that was sufficient but specifically Bakunin, or the "Bakunin-principle" as the "essential valid stimulus for effective action," expressed as "I destroy and I build."

Despite Stephensen's affiliation with the Communist Party and his positive references to Lenin and Trotsky in the same essay, he points out that Bakunin rejected communism as no better than capitalism. Nor was Stephensen under any illusions about the contemporary anarchists who had become irrelevant "entirely." Rather, Stephensen cites Bakunin and Herzen who theorized early on that socialism would triumph, but it would

---

[13] Stephensen, "Bakunin," Part I.
[14] Stephensen, "Bakunin," Part VIII.
[15] Stephensen, "Bakunin," Part XI.

make way for "a revolution unknown to us," as part of a dialectical "flux and re-flux of history . . . the *perpetuum mobile* of life." Stephensen regarded this as "the soundest possible revolutionary theory."[16]

Stephensen's polemic against Christianity was also a Nietzschean-revolutionary synthesis, expressed in a poem entitled "Holy Smoke."[17] He challenges God to perform a miracle to make believers in an unbelieving age:

> . . . No answer. Sulk the felon stretching taut
> Your wooden muscles on the gallows-tree,
> Worshipped by sniveling women and masochists—
> Abandon us in your abstract Kingdom of Heaven!
> Keep your eternal Bliss!—I'm off to hell
> To tempt the devil to place some orders for coal
> In Britain, to relieve unemployment; even though
> The devil is beyond temptation, being a Bolshevik . . .
>
> —The Bishop will preach tonight to exhortation
> To follow the Golden Rule, or the Rule of Gold . . .

Stephensen continues with his inquisitorial reproach, asking why Jesus did not strike back at the authorities in the Garden of Gethsemane:

> . . . —But grant us, Old Gods of the North, to resist our foes,
> Returning a stronger blow for each blow received!
> Grant us hate with passion in our blood,
> Grant us the death of heroes, unforgiving,
> And failing a rescue, let us die with a curse . . .

This aversion to Christianity is not noticeable in Stephensen's later political activities and writings in Australia. However, it is reasonable to think that it helped form a basis for co-operation

---

[16] Stephensen, "Bakunin," Part XVI.
[17] Stephensen, "Holy Smoke: An Essay in Religious Experience," ca. 1928.

between Stephensen and the Sydney businessman W. J. Miles, a prominent rationalist who funded Stephensen's cultural and political nationalism, including the launching of *The Publicist*.

PUBLISHING

In 1927 Stephensen took over the Fanfrolico Press which specialized in limited editions, along with the literary journal the *London Aphrodite*.[18] He went on to establish the Mandrake Press and published a book reproducing paintings by D. H. Lawrence, Lawrence's *Apropos of Lady Chatterley's Lover*, and a volume of Lawrence's poems, *Pansies*.[19] Stephensen also helped to publish an underground edition of Lawrence's *Lady Chatterley's Lover*, which was the first edition to be printed in England.

Stephensen's innate rebelliousness is also displayed by his writing and publishing a biography of the infamous occultist and poet Aleister Crowley, who the sensationalist press was describing at the time as "the wickedest man in the world," "The King of Depravity," and "A Man We'd Like to Hang."[20] Stephensen had no interest in occultism or mysticism *per se*. As with his support for D. H. Lawrence, his work on Crowley was probably motivated by the latter's opposition to bourgeois society. Crowley's Nietzschean-style polemics against Christianity would also have appealed to Stephensen.

Israel Regardie, Crowley's secretary at the time and a lifelong devotee, wrote years later in the "Introduction" to Stephensen's biography of Crowley that Stephensen and his wife, a classical ballerina, were "very charming and kind people. . . . Inky's interest in Aleister Crowley was wholly literary. He had a good grounding in philosophy, but cared absolutely nothing for the occult."[21] Stephensen, for his part, regarded Crowley as a literary "genius."[22] Considering the furor around Crowley at

---

[18] *The Puzzled Patriots*, p. 21.

[19] *The Puzzled Patriots*, p. 22.

[20] Sandy Robertson, *The Aleister Crowley Scrapbook* (London: W. Foulsham, 1988), p. 7.

[21] Israel Regardie, "Introduction," 1969; P. R. Stephensen, *The Confessions of Aleister Crowley*, 1930 (Phoenix, Arizona: Falcon Press, 1983).

[22] Stephensen, *The Confessions of Aleister Crowley*, pp. 13–14. Ste-

the time, it is indicative of Stephensen's disregard of conformity, which would re-emerge in his political activities when the Axis powers were widely perceived as evil incarnate.

Stephensen's Mandrake Press also published Crowley's novels *Moonchild* and *The Stratagem*, and the first two volumes of a projected six-volume *Confessions of Aleister Crowley*, the third volume of which never got as far as proofreading.[23] Stephensen wrote the biography in order to try and mitigate the damage done to the sales of Crowley's books as a result of bad publicity about Crowley's character, something which was hardly helped by the self-styled "Great Beast's" own cultivation of notoriety.[24] However, the biography did not sell well, *The Confessions* was boycotted by booksellers,[25] and Mandrake Press was liquidated.[26]

AUSTRALIAN NATIONALIST

Stephensen's eight-year stay in England seems to have been influential in making him an Australian nationalist. Perhaps it was a simple matter of homesickness. In any case, he left in 1932, feeling that Britain was headed for "inevitable decline" in which he saw possibility of "an Australian resurgence."[27] Settling in Sydney, Stephensen resumed his publishing career as managing director of the Endeavour Press (funded by the *Bulletin* magazine) and turned out more than 30 volumes of Australian literature.[28] Stephensen's attempts to launch his own publishing ventures were financially unsuccessful, although he had become a recognized figure in Australian literature and vice-president of the Fellowship of Australian Writers. He was also by now advocating what he called "Australia First."[29]

---

phensen asked that Crowley be judged by his poetry and prose and not by his notorious character.

[23] *The Aleister Crowley Scrapbook*, p. 19.
[24] Regardie, "Introduction," pp. ii–iii.
[25] *The Aleister Crowley Scrapbook*, p. 19.
[26] Regardie, "Introduction," p. v.
[27] *The Puzzled Patriots*, p. 24.
[28] *The Puzzled Patriots*, p. 25.
[29] *The Puzzled Patriots*, p. 28.

Foundations of Australian Culture

In July 1935 Stephensen published *The Foundations of Culture in Australia: An Essay Towards National Self Respect*.[30] It is a vigorous call for an Australian national culture, which has remained influential in literary circles although seldom acknowledged as such.

Stephensen, despite his own defense of the Aborigines and his opposition to Australian colonial "cultural cringe," states as one of his first axioms that Australian culture begins with the arrival of the British. From this rich heritage of Europe could arise a uniquely Australian culture which would evolve by the impress of "Time and Place":

> As the culture of every nation is an intellectual and emotional expression of the *genius loci*, our Australian culture will diverge from the purely local color of the British Islands, to the precise extent that our environment differs from that of Britain. A hemisphere separates us from "home." We are Antipodeans; a gum tree is not a branch of an oak; our Australia culture will evolve distinctively.
>
> ... what is a national culture? Is it not the expression, in thought form, of art-form, of the Spirit of a Race and of a Place?
>
> It is culture that provides "permanence" for a nation while all else moves on. Culture transcends "modernism" and the ephemeral nature of politics, society, and economics. Race and Place are the two permanent elements in a culture, and Place, I think, is even more important than Race in giving that culture its direction. When races migrate, taking their culture with them, to a new Place, the culture becomes modified. It is the spirit of a Place that ultimately gives any human culture its distinctiveness.

---

[30] Stephensen, *The Foundations of Culture in Australia: An Essay Towards National Self Respect* (Gordon, New South Wales: W. J. Miles, 1936). Percy Stephensen Collection:
http://home.alphalink.com.au/~radnat/stephensen/prs4.html

It is literature, according to Stephensen, that gives the greatest sense of Place and Race and Permanence to a nation and which indeed creates the nation. Robert Burns is an example of the way Scotland as an "idea" is expressed. With England, it is Chaucer, Shakespeare, and Dickens, more so than the politicians, merchants and soldiers. The "idea" of the French nation has been likewise expressed through Montaigne, Rabelais, Voltaire, Victor Hugo, and Balzac. Germany lives in Goethe, Heine, Kant, Hegel, and Richard Wagner. Russia has Dostoevsky, Tolstoy, Chekhov, Maxim Gorky; Scandinavia, Ibsen and Knut Hamsun.

However, in the case of Australia, art was more reflective of an emerging Australian culture than was its literature. Early Australian literature based around the *Bulletin* magazine, and epitomized by poets and writers such as Henry Lawson, was of a rough nature because it was a radical response to British denigration of Australians as "convicts."

Landscape painting in Australia, however, was never based on a journalistic element. Landscape painters had to examine Australia carefully, expressing "the Spirit of the Place," the strange contours of the land, the solitude, and the light quality of the atmosphere that symbolize most purely what is Australian. Australian painters were also dependent upon a national audience and market, not a world market where art is prostituted for money. The painting is individual, while the book is mass produced.

Although art can be appreciated internationally it is "nationally created," "formed locally no matter how it might travel." Regardless of how travel and communication break down barriers, local cultures remain. A creative thinker contributes to the culture of his own people first, and then to the culture of the world. But a writer or an artist needs the stimulus of his own people.

Despite the universalizing tendencies at work, Australia had the right to become a nation, but there cannot be a nation without "a national place idea, a national culture." Stephensen's view of culture as "national" rather than "universal" was widely held by the culture-bearing strata throughout the world. It is also strictly analogous to the sentiments of Rex Fairburn in

New Zealand, in response to the communist fad among many contemporaries.

Stephensen attacks those academics who sought to demean Australia as a nation and as a culture by forever subordinating Australia to Britain and to the British Empire. He acknowledges that it is English culture from which Australian culture will proceed. But it is the growing plant, rather than the English fertilizer, that should now be of concern. Culture is the essence of nationality, and the nation an extension of the individuals that comprise it "generation after generation." Nationality gives the individual a sense of pride and meaning.

Stephensen draws on a cyclical Spenglerian understanding of history in holding that nations and empires undergo decline over the course of centuries. Stephensen's Spenglerianism was also reflected in an essay in which the cyclic paradigm is used to show that the British Empire, like any other, was subjected to historical laws of rise and fall. He foretells Britain's decline during the twentieth century, and maintains that on its ruins Australia would find its own identity and destiny:

> History is the tale of waxing and waning empires. All empires have waxed before waning. Britain's Empire has waxed — will it now wane? Yes, inevitably. An empire is no more permanent than an oak-tree: the mightiest oak must fall, rotting hollow at the core. Everything that has life in it has death in it, too. A moment of rapture, or a moment of power, cannot be prolonged unduly beyond its zenith. Where there has been strength and greatness, there must come sequent decline and fall. Without deaths, there would be no births. Death is necessary, to make way for more life. Old empires, old cultures, must crash — and Britain's Empire with them — to make way for new empires, new cultures. Who would have it otherwise? Only those who object to death's inevitability and to time's changes! Let them object — the objection is noted — and history's blind processes go on.[31]

---

[31] Stephensen, "Decline and Fall of the British Empire: An Australi-

Bruce Muirden, for reasons unknown, states that *Foundations* "was probably to be [Stephensen's] final public statement as a liberal." And Stephensen was even then referring to fascism as more a danger to Australia than Bolshevism ever could be (he regarded Bolshevism as "at least [having] a humanitarian goal"[32]). Nonetheless, *Foundations* is unmistakably of the "Right," with its emphasis on the "spirit of race and place," that has no association with the Left, let alone with "liberalism." This Rightist orientation was soon to be reflected in Stephensen's new political associations, which he maintained for the rest of his life.

THE PUBLICIST

W. J. Miles was a wealthy businessman whose First World War activities included opposition to conscription and advocacy of the concept of "Australia First." In 1935, he contacted Stephensen after reading *Foundations*. Together they launched a magazine, *The Publicist*, which lasted until 1942. It was described as "the paper loyal to Australia First." Miles was in editorial control, and his views were overtly pro-Axis. German, Italian, and Japanese propaganda material was sold at the *Publicist* offices.[33] A free hand for Japan in China was supported at a time when the Left was calling for a boycott of Japan.[34]

Stephensen viewed Japan as "the only country in the world completely free of international Jew Finance."[35] He believed that there would be a world war involving Australia within a few years. He saw no advantage to Australia in sending her men to spill their blood in Europe.[36] Many Australians remembered the huge losses suffered during World War I caused in part by the unrealistic orders of British commanders. Already in 1936 *The Publicist* was running a satirical recruiting poster

---

an Nationalist Point of View,"
http://home.alphalink.com.au/~radnat/stephensen/prs8.html

[32] *The Puzzled Patriots*, p. 28.
[33] *The Puzzled Patriots*, p. 36.
[34] *The Puzzled Patriots*, p. 37.
[35] *The Puzzled Patriots*, p. 37.
[36] *The Puzzled Patriots*, p. 39.

referring to the coming "Great European War": "Don't Go Your Country Needs You. Australia will be Here."[37] In 1939, as the crisis in Europe was fast approaching, Stephensen wrote, "Why need Australians bemoan the absorption of Czechoslovakia by Germany when Australia is already 'absorbed' by British and American Jew-Capitalists?"

Despite the radical tone of Miles and Stephensen, *The Publicist* attracted a number of prominent cultural figures, such as Ian Mudie and Rex Ingamells,[38] who wrote on the arts. It also offered a generous amount of space to its enemies for right of reply. In 1939 Stephensen advocated the need for a heroic leader, "a man of harsh vitality, a born leader, a man of action, no what sicklied o'er with the pale cast of thought. Fanatics are needed, crude harsh men, not sweetened and decorous men, to arouse us from the lethargy of decadence, softness and lies which threatens death to white Australia."[39]

Democracy was part of the weakness and decay of the modern world. In a radio talk in 1938 Stephensen stated, "We oppose democracy as a political system, because we believe it can never evolve the bold leadership that will be necessary to guide Australia through the difficulties of the coming year."[40]

TOWARDS A PARTY

Between 1936 and 1937 *The Publicist* started putting forward broad points of policy for the establishment of an Australia First Party.[41] In 1938 readers' groups suggested a twelve-point program as a basis for discussion. The principal group was the Yabber Club in Sydney, whose attendees included Mudie.[42]

---

[37] *The Puzzled Patriots*, p. 39.

[38] Founder of the cultural-nationalist *Jindyworobak* movement in 1938, upon which Stephensen's *Foundations* had had a seminal influence, although Ingamells thought that Stephensen conceded too much to British influence on the development of Australian identity. *The Puzzled Patriots*, p. 51.

[39] Stephensen, *The Publicist*, July 1939.

[40] Stephensen, December 12, 1938.

[41] *The Puzzled Patriots*, pp. 42–43.

[42] *The Puzzled Patriots*, pp. 44–46. A selection of his poems written in

When war was declared, the Australian authorities began to scrutinize the Yabber Club, but their informants could find nothing sinister about it.

In the September issue of *The Publicist*, Stephensen stated that he had campaigned for peace with Germany, since any war Australia fought should be for Australian rather than Jewish interests.[43] *The Publicist* was now subjected to wartime censorship and paper restrictions. However, only one article, and not one by Stephensen,[44] was ever blocked by the authorities. This indicates that *The Publicist* was not considered subversive by the censorship board. Naturally, the Left was not so charitable, and referred to *The Publicist* as the center of a "Nazi Underworld," although the position of the Communists at this stage of the war was hardly intended to be helpful to the Allies.

While the pro-Germany sentiments had to be toned down during 1940, *The Publicist* maintained its friendly attitude towards Japan. Once Australia was engaged in the war with Japan, the journal opposed any defeatist tendencies but continued to advocate home defense rather than sending Australian troops far afield, and the right to negotiate independently and to sue for a separate peace.

After several years of tentative activities Stephensen formed the Australia First Movement in September 1941. A major element in the formation of the movement was the Sydney Women's Guild of Empire, formerly antagonistic towards *The Publicist* due to the issue of loyalty to Britain. The mainstay of the Guild was Adele Pankhurst Walsh of the British suffragette family. On migrating to Australia, she had married the militant Seamen's Union organizer Tom Walsh in 1917. Both became founding members of the Australian Communist Party. Breaking with communism, Tom joined and lectured for the "New Guard"[45] and was outspokenly pro-Japanese.[46]

1942 can be found at: http://home.alphalink.com.au/~radnat/mudie.html

[43] *The Puzzled Patriots*, p. 49.
[44] *The Puzzled Patriots*, p. 50.
[45] The New Guard was established by Eric Campbell in 1931, pri-

A ten-point manifesto was adopted, superseding Stephensen's more radical manifesto of 1940. The movement demanded recall of Australian troops from overseas, independent action in diplomacy, and the removal of American influence.[47]

A number of public meetings involved hecklers. However, a meeting in February 1942, which had an audience of around 300, erupted into what the press termed "one of the worst brawls ever to occur in a Sydney public hall." Half the audience was antagonistic, and Stephensen in particular was met

---

marily to oppose communism and specifically the New South Wales Labour government of Jack Lang, reaching a membership of 50,000. Ironically, it was Lang, in the tradition of Old Labour, who was staunchly anti-communist, a die-hard advocate of "White Australia," and of particular significance, advocated suspension of interest payments to British bondholders, interest on government bond holdings to be reduced from 6% to 3%, and the issue of state credit based on the "goods standard," not the "gold standard." Keith Amos, *The New Guard Movement 1931–1935* (Carlton, Victoria: Melbourne University Press, 1976), p. 23.

While the New Guard had the trappings of fascism such as the Roman salute, Campbell did not consider fascism as a doctrine until 1933 when he visited Mussolini. In hindsight, it could be contended that it was Lang who from the start was a thoroughly-grounded Australian Nationalist rather than the paramilitary Empire patriots who wished to defend British and Australian bondholders. Additionally, the "Lang Plan" was of more specifically nationalist orientation than the free trade economics of Stephensen. See also: Jack Lang, "White Australia Saved Australia," *I Remember* (1956), Chapter 6.

Stephensen did have a perceptive view about the New Guard in pointing out that Lang's dismissal from Office was supported by the "pseudo-Fascist New Guard": "Peculiar Fascists are these led by Eric Campbell, using the Fascist technique not for a National cause (as in Germany or Italy), but for the cause of International (British) finance." Stephensen, "A Brief Survey of Australia History: Our Story in Fifteen Decades," (1938), The Percy Stephensen Collection, http://home.alphalink.com.au/~radnat/stephensen/index.html

[46] *The Puzzled Patriots*, p. 60. Mrs. Walsh was soon asked to withdraw from the movement because of her overly enthusiastic support for Japan.

[47] *The Puzzled Patriots*, p. 62.

with opposition. He was hit over the head with a water carafe, knocked to the floor, and kicked by a group. The police were slow to respond. However, once order was established, Stephensen continued with the meeting despite the beating, and continuing interjections. Stephensen addressed the meeting for around eighty minutes. He demanded that American troops in Australia be subject to Australian command and stated that they should be there to protect Australia, not to further American objectives.[48]

On orders from the Attorney General Dr. Evatt, the police prevented Australia First from holding further public meetings. At a later meeting, a crowd of 3000 showed up to listen to Stephensen, only to find the meeting canceled by government directive.[49]

STEPHENSEN'S POLITICAL DEMANDS

Because the movement was now unable to have public meetings, Stephensen regretted that it would have to exist as, in effect, a social club until after the war. Stephensen's ideas for a post-war party included policies more far-ranging and elaborate than anything hitherto printed in *The Publicist*. In particular, they convey Stephensen's aversion to democracy as causing party and economic divisions, appealing to the lowest common denominator for vote-catching purposes, undermining leadership, avoiding responsibility, and leading to "decay."

Stephensen posited his 50-point manifesto for an Australia First Party to be founded after the war, in the May 1, 1940 issue of *The Publicist*. This was presented as a series of for-and-against propositions. For example:

> 6. For national socialism; against international communism.
> [...]
> 14. For higher birth-rate; against immigration.
> 15. For "White" Australia; against heterogeneity.

---

[48] *The Puzzled Patriots*, pp. 66–68.
[49] *The Puzzled Patriots*, p. 69.

16. For Aryanism; against Semitism.
[...]
35. For women in the home; against women in industry.[50]

On August 1, 1941 under the heading "Towards a New Order," it was stated that these were principles, not planks, for a democratic parliamentary party. The article was an explication of the Fifty-Point program of May 1940. "Our self-imposed task was to throw a stone into the stagnant pond of Australian political complacency," Stephensen writes in the preamble. He states that the war gave birth to the need for forms of government other than democracy, despite the war supposedly being fought for democracy. The war aims made sectional interests redundant in the service of the common interest.[51] This perception had formed the basis of fascist movements after the First World War among many returned servicemen, in what Mosley called "the socialism of the trenches," a camaraderie of soldiers that many held should be brought over into peacetime civil life. The aftermath of the Second World War, however, did not see another revival of that spirit for reasons that cannot detain us here.

The first three points call for Australian cultural and political self-reliance, against imitating ideas from abroad and dependency upon others. A "distinctive national Australian culture" is regarded as the prerequisite for "National Unity, National Consciousness, and National Survival." The fourth point calls for "nationalism, against internationalism." Nations are natural political units defined by racial and political factors.

Point 6 favors "national socialism, against international communism." However, Stephensen repudiates any monopoly of the term National Socialism by Germany. "We support all NATIONAL forms of socialism, as against the international version of socialism favored by Marxism." In those sectors of the

---

[50] Stephensen, "Fifty Points of Policy for an Australia-First Party After the War," *The Publicist*, May 1, 1940, http://home.alphalink.com.au/~radnat/stephensen/index.html

[51] Stephensen, "Towards a New Order," *The Publicist*, August 1, 1941, http://home.alphalink.com.au/~radnat/stephensen/prs2.html

economy where private interests would become a power over the nation, the state would be required to intervene.

Further points call for frankness and honesty in diplomacy, with a "live and let live" attitude minus the moralizing towards others that leads to war. The emphasis on defense was about protecting Australia, rather than serving other interests overseas. An attitude of friendliness was to be fostered towards nations bordering the Pacific Ocean, which could only be achieved when Australia was not subordinate militarily and diplomatically to British or other interests.

Stephensen considers a declining birth rate a symptom of decadence which would lead to the extinction of Australia, especially when there were suggestions to make up for the population shortfall through immigration, one of the panaceas for demographic decline that is now routinely touted by politicians in Australia and New Zealand. He called for a white Australia as a "biological aim" to create a permanent home for persons of "European racial derivation." This would exclude "Semites" and other non-absorbable immigrants.

However, Stephensen's championship of "Aryanism" cannot be dismissed as simple racial supremacism. Stephensen was an avid supporter of Aborigine rights, serving as secretary of the Aborigines' Citizenship Committee, which supported the Aborigines' Progressive Association comprised of an Aborigine only membership. The *Abo Call* was a magazine that sold in the *Publicist* office alongside the Axis journals. Stephensen helped Aborigines organize the "Aborigine's Day of Mourning" on January 26, 1939, the 150th anniversary of the "founding of Australia."[52] The sympathy of Australian nationalists with the Aborigine, decades before the issue became a cliché for liberals and "progressives" of all types, was seen by such cultural nationalists as an essential part of formulating a *mythos* of the nature of Australia that harks back to its earliest days of settlement as a unique southern continent. It was a matter of particular interest to Rex Ingamell's cultural-nationalist *Jindyworobak* movement, which had an informal association with Australia First.

---

[52] *The Puzzled Patriots*, pp. 47–48.

Introducing women into the workplace and away from child-bearing under the name of "feminism" is attacked as leading to the decline in the birth-rate as well as undermining the wage standard.

Much of the rest of the manifesto is an attack on the democratic and parliamentary system. Interestingly, in this light, despite Stephensen's aversion to British and other outside influence, he upheld hereditary monarchy rather than the idea of a republic with an elected head of state. Stephensen desired a government of statesmen with firm, long-term principles, as opposed to short-term vote pandering by political parties leading to compromise and demagoguery rather than the sometimes-harsh policies required for survival. Despite a specifically Australian nationalism, monarchy could reasonably be seen as the best form of government suited to the idea of "permanence," rather than petty political transience.

The means of achieving this unity and strength was through "Corporatism," a form of government that was attracting widespread support from around the world during the 1930s as a means of overcoming the crisis of capitalism while avoiding the destructiveness of communism. Corporatism had become the system of government under which Fascist Italy functioned, where the democratic party structure of parliament was replaced by chambers of corporations representing the crafts and professions. Corporatism also agreed with Catholic social doctrine, and certain "fascist" parties in some countries took specifically Catholic forms, such as Rexism in Belgium, Hungarism in Hungary, the Irish Blueshirts, Adrien Arcand's movement in Canada, etc. Corporatism was seen at the time by many as the wave of the future, and corporatist regimes formed in Brazil, Portugal, Austria, and Italy before the war. Stephensen also refers to the Corporate State as, "the Body Politic" and the "Social Organism," "A political idea as old as humanity, a biological fact as old as organic life."[53]

The organic social order had existed until the French and American Revolutions. Stephensen explains how these up-

---

[53] Stephensen, "Towards a New Order, Point 26, National Unity."

heavals undermined the traditional social order with "democratic sectionalism," and "an alleged equality inspired by the thoughts of J.-J. Rousseau," the Swiss philosopher. The result, under the facade of democracy and equality, was not to empower "the people," but to empower industrial and financial interests which are able to use democracy to undermine any authority and power. However, Corporatism enables the social organism to function as "an integral whole" subjecting sectional interests, whether class or party, to the interests of the community, like the cells of a biological organism that all function for the common good of the whole.

While Stephensen believed this Corporatist or organic state was necessary to bring harmony between the social and economic classes, and expected both capital and labor to restrain their sectional demands for the benefit of the whole, his ideas on financial and economic policy do not seem to have been well developed. Despite his opposition to "international Jew finance," as he put it, and his recognition that the Axis countries had thrown off the power of the plutocrats, his statements on policy do not reflect a recognition that the Axis economies were based on state regulation of credit and currency creation and a system of trade based on barter. Instead, Stephensen opts for more orthodox banking practices and condemns theories of credit expansion and specifically Social Credit, to which many like-minded men of letters such as Ezra Pound and T. S. Eliot adhered as a means of overthrowing the rule of money. Hence the points on economics in the 50-point program include:

44. For industrial development; against speculation.
45. For competition; against monopoly.
46. For private ownership; against government encroachment.
47. For conservative banking practice; against inflation.
48. For less taxation; against greater taxation.
49. For reduction of debt; against increase of debt.
50. For world trade; against restricted trade.[54]

---

[54] Stephensen, "Fifty Point of Policy for an Australia-First Party Af-

He does, however, expect capitalists to invest their capital in productive rather than speculative enterprises once the state has ensured an economic climate generating reasonable returns for such investment. His opposition to debt, increased taxation, and speculation, nonetheless failed to tackle the root cause of these factors in the economy. This was the debt-finance system, and many nationalists of the time recognized the necessity of replacing it with an alternative system such as C. H. Douglas' Social Credit, or state credit, endorsed by Ezra Pound, Rex Fairburn, etc. His primary platform on banking referred to: "conservative banking practice; against inflation." The inadequacy of this financial policy is all the more remarkable considering that in Australia at the time, as in New Zealand, Social Credit had a popular following. State credit had also been a major demand in the Australian Labour movement, as it had in New Zealand, where the iconic "state housing project" had provided work for 75% of the unemployed by the use of 1% state credit.[55]

STEPHENSEN'S "REASONED CASE AGAINST SEMITISM"

Stephensen, like other Rightist men of letters such as Ezra Pound, retained friendships with Jews as individuals but expressed animosity towards a perceived Jewish political agenda and regarded Jews as an unassimilable minority. His partner in Mandrake Press was Jewish, Edward Goldston, as was his collaborator on the Crowley biography, Israel Regardie, who was to retain a life-long affectionate memory of "Inky."[56]

Stephensen presented his "Reasoned Case Against Semitism" in 1940 in *The Australian Quarterly*. He states that anti-Semitism arises as an anti-toxin to the toxin of an aggressive "pro-Semitism." His concern with the Jewish question seems to have been particularly prompted by a suggestion that a territo-

---

ter the War."

[55] K. R. Bolton, "State Credit and Reconstruction: The First New Zealand Labour Government," *Journal for the Study of Social Economics*, Vol. 38, No. 1, February 2011.

[56] Regardie, "Introduction."

ry in northwest Australia be set aside for Jewish refugees from Europe. Stephensen opposed any "cessation" of Australian land.

He saw in the Jews a highly-organized, separatist minority which pursued its own interests. The Jews remain a separate minority by choice, indeed by their insistence as a "God-Chosen People." Stephensen states that "they cannot have it both ways"—being treated as no different to anyone else, while insisting on remaining aloof from the nation in which they reside. Their propaganda includes agitation for internationalism and the concept of the "Universal Oneness of Mankind" among Gentiles, yet they have maintained themselves through 5000 years by a most exclusivistic racialism. Stephensen states that nobody likes being "humbugged" with such a double standard.

Stephensen compares the manner by which a small number of Jews are able to wield immense influence through a superior close-knit communal organization to the manner by which communist cells were able to insinuate themselves into institutions and get their measures adopted by an unsuspecting and mostly lethargic majority. The "too-zealous propagandists of the Jewish Cause" in Australia had done the Jews a disservice by drawing attention to the them as a distinct community, for anti-Semitism is a reaction to aggressive pro-Semitism and neither exists unless a nation is in a pathological state.

To Stephensen, exclusion of Jewish immigrants is simply a continuation of the White Australia policy that had been a mainstay for the development of Australian nationhood, based on the aim of what he calls "Fused-European Homogeneity." European migrants had discarded their Old-World ties and amalgamated to form what was becoming an Australian nationality. Australia had "antedated Hitler's 'racial theories' by fifty years."

It is of interest that the White Australia policy was not of imperial or capitalistic origin but was instead one of the primary aims of the Australian Labour movement, which met principal opposition from both the British Colonial Office and from Australian business interests which sought a pool of coolie labor.⁵⁷ The demand for immigration restriction was an *ideal* – a *nation-building mythos* – that shaped Australian identity, albeit one that was predictably subverted in recent decades by the bourgeois Left (antithetical to "Old Labour") in tandem with Big Business.⁵⁸ Among the most memorable advocates of the policy were the working-class literati, such as the poet Henry Lawson, and also William Lane, founder of the Australian Labor Federation. In pre-emption of Stephensen, Lane stated: "We are for this Australia, for the nationality which is creeping on the verge of being . . . Here we face the hordes of the east as our kinsmen faced them in the dim distant past . . ."⁵⁹

Should Jews forego their Jewishness and fully integrate and intermarry there would be no Jewish problem. That they do not do so is their choice, but Stephensen was convinced that they would never forsake their Jewishness, and so the Jewish problem would remain. "Here then we are faced with a defiance by Jews of the fundamental principle of Fused-European Homogeneity which it is the basic aim of Australian national policy to establish and maintain. They claim the right not only to settle here but to maintain themselves in perpetuity, as a self-segregated minority, of different and distinct racial stock from the rest of the Australian community."⁶⁰ It is, as he points out, a matter of perspective. As a non-Jew in any conflict of interest between Jew and Gentile he would instinctively side with his own. Stephensen's loyalty was to Australia, and a large migration of Jewish refugees from Europe would undermine the Australia that he wished to see developing as a nation, culture, and people on its own account.

INTERNMENT

Such sentiments were regarded as treasonous by the authorities whose government had tied Australia to British imperial

---

⁵⁷ Jack Lang, "White Australia Saved Australia."

⁵⁸ K. R. Bolton, *Babel Inc.: Multiculturalism, Globalisation and the New World Order* (London: Black House Publishing, 2013).

⁵⁹ William Lane, *The Boomerang: A Live Newspaper Born of the Soil*, March 17, 1888.

⁶⁰ Stephensen, "A Reasoned Case Against Semitism."

and American, i.e., plutocratic, interests. Additionally, several individuals and groups had gained the attention of military intelligence as possible collaborators in the event of a Japanese invasion.[61] Some of these were loosely connected to the Australia First Movement.

"Enemy aliens," including those who were anti-fascist, were being interned.[62] Sixteen supporters of the Australia First movement, whom the press described as a "spy ring,"[63] including Stephensen and his brother Eric, were detained under Regulation 26 at Liverpool internment camp in March 1942. Police occupied the *Publicist* office. The poet and author Ian Mudie, an executive member of the movement, was questioned but not interned, although he was to remark that he was either as "guilty" or "innocent" as those who were. Muirden comments: "Strangely, the *Publicist* was not banned, and the movement was not officially proscribed."[64] However, this was unnecessary, and perhaps could be regarded as being hypocritical, since Stephensen, and the other two proprietors of *The Publicist* were interned with key members.

The Bulletin remained strongly opposed to the internments, and made much of one of the internees being "an Old Digger." The latter, Martin Watts, a holder of the Military Medal from the First World War, was conditionally released after a few months along with several others. However, Watts's job was gone, and he died several weeks later of bronchial pneumonia, exacerbated by his internment.[65] The internees were questioned

---

[61] What one might whimsically call the "collaborationist conspiracy" in Australia centered around government agent "Hardt," and a couple of individuals who were not aligned to Australia First; Nancy Krakouer (of Jewish descent), Laurence Bullock, and E. C. Quicke, harmless dreamers, who thought they might form a collaborationist government in the event of a Japanese invasion. Authorities were not able to establish any association between these and Australia First. *The Puzzled Patriots*, p. 144.

[62] *The Puzzled Patriots*, p. 94.

[63] *The Puzzled Patriots*, p. 110.

[64] *The Puzzled Patriots*, p. 113.

[65] *The Puzzled Patriots*, p. 113. His wife Dora, who was part Jewish,

before a secret tribunal, and no record was kept of proceedings, although one internee did manage to record the questions. Despite Australia First never having been banned, the questions directed at the internees make it plain that they were being persecuted because of their association with the movement. [66]

Transferred to Loveday Camp, then to Tatura Camp, Stephensen spent three-and-a-half years interned.[67]

After the war, several ex-internees continued to campaign for exoneration, and two issued a reprint of the 1942 issues of the *Publicist* to provide a "durable historical record" that would show their loyalty and patriotism.

POST-WAR

Ian Mudie had been keen to see Australia First revived. However, Stephensen was optimistic regarding the development of Australia's national consciousness and believed the aims of the movement were being realized. The imperial connection was dissipating, and there was a growing interest in Australian culture.

For the first decade after the war Stephensen was mainly involved in assisting Australian writers, principally Frank Clune.[68] By 1959 Stephensen had sufficiently re-established his literary reputation to be asked to undertake a Commonwealth Literary Fund lecture tour of South Australia with Mudie. The lectures were published as *Nationalism in Australian Literature*.[69] Other such lectures followed in Queensland in 1961.[70] By this time, his continuing theme of an Australian national culture was meeting with wider support.

---

was to maintain lifelong activity in the Australian "Right." As late as 1978 she was writing for an Australian nationalist periodical. Dora Watts, "The Murder of a Nation," *Advance!,* no. 4, January–February 1978, p. 7.

[66] *The Puzzled Patriots*, p. 122.
[67] *The Puzzled Patriots*, p. 128.
[68] *The Puzzled Patriots*, p. 177.
[69] Stephensen, *Nationalism in Australian Literature* (Adelaide: Commonwealth Literary Fund Lecture, 1959).
[70] *The Puzzled Patriots*, p. 178.

Stephensen's literary output continued at an impressive rate, and included *The Viking of Van Diemen's Land*,[71] *The Cape Horn Breed*,[72] *Sail Ho!*,[73] *Sydney Sails*,[74] *The Pirates of the Brig Cyprus*,[75] and *The History and Description of Sydney Harbour*.[76] His seminal *Foundations of Culture in Australia* was republished in 1986.[77]

Stephensen collapsed and died on May 28, 1965 after giving a lively address on *Lady Chatterley's Lover*.[78] He never moderated his beliefs.

Counter-Currents/ *North American New Right*
November 20, 2011

---

[71] *The Viking of Van Diemen's Land* (Sydney: Angus & Robertson, 1954).

[72] *The Cape Horn Breed*, with William H. S. Jones (London: Andrew Melrose, 1956).

[73] *Sail Ho!*, with Sir James Bisset (London: Rupert Hart-Davis, 1961) and several other books with Sir James.

[74] *Sydney Sails: The Story of the Royal Sydney Yacht Squadron's First 100 years* (Sydney: Angus & Robertson, 1962).

[75] *The Pirates of the Brig Cyprus*, with Frank Clune (London: Rupert Hart-Davis, 1962).

[76] *The History and Description of Sydney Harbour*, with Brian Kennedy (Adelaide: Rigby, 1966).

[77] *Foundations of Culture in Australia* (Sydney: George Allen & Unwin, 1986).

[78] *The Puzzled Patriots*, p. 180.

Chapter 5

Rex Fairburn

A. R. D. "Rex" Fairburn, 1904–1957, is not usually identified with the "Right." As a central figure in the development of a New Zealand national literature, much of the contemporary self-appointed literary establishment would no doubt wish to identify Fairburn with Marxism or liberalism, as they would other leading literary friends of Fairburn's such as the communist R. A. K. Mason. However, the primary influences on Fairburn were distinctly non-Left, and include D. H. Lawrence, Nietzsche, Oswald Spengler, and of course Social Credit's Major C. H. Douglas.

While Fairburn described himself at times as an "anarchist,"[1] it was of a most unorthodox type, being neither Left-wing nor Libertarian. Fairburn outspokenly rejected all the baggage dear to the Left, including feminism and internationalism. His "anarchism" was a type of Right-wing individualism that called for a return to decentralized communities comprised of self-reliant craftsmen and farmers. His creed was distinctly nationalistic and based on the spiritual and the biological components of history and culture, both concepts being antithetical to any form of Leftism.

We feel more than justified, then, in identifying Fairburn as an "Artist of the Right."

The Rejection of Rationalism

Fairburn was born in modest but middle-class circumstances. He was proud of being a fourth-generation New Zealander related to the missionary Colenso. Although critical of the church hierarchy and briefly involved with the Rationalist As-

---

[1] Fairburn to R. A. K. Mason, December 28, 1931, cited by Denys Trussell, *Fairburn* (Auckland: Auckland University Press, 1984), p. 116.

sociation, Fairburn was for most of his life a spiritual person, believing that the individual becomes most profoundly who he is by striving towards God. He believed in a basic Christian ethic minus any moralism. Fairburn soon realized that rationalism by itself answers nothing and that it rejects the dream world that is the source of creativity. He was in agreement here with other poets of the Right such as Yeats, and throughout his life often stated his rejection of materialism.

While he agreed with his friend Geoffrey Potocki de Montalk, who called poets a "spiritual aristocracy," Fairburn at first thought socialism was the way to "free artists of economic, worldly shackles," and even made sporadic favorable references to Communism.[2] However, he looked in particular to the non-doctrinaire socialism not of a political theorist but of another artistic luminary, Oscar Wilde, whose essay on the subject[3] he enthusiastically recommended to Potocki. Wilde advocating the elimination of the "burden" of private property to free the creative spirit from economic drudgery.[4]

Potocki would have no belief in socialism of any type other than "national socialism," and Fairburn would find the answer to the economic question he was looking for in Social Credit. Nonetheless, these early socialist interests were part of Fairburn's quest for a more humane system.

Throughout his life, Fairburn rejected any form of materialism and rationalism, and it seems likely that in his youth he had not realized that these are features of communism and of most forms of socialism, given his rather romantic ideal of "socialism" and even of Communism. Fairburn came to see the counting-house mentality as intrinsic to rationalism and it repelled his sense of the spiritual.

He wrote of this counting-house mentality,

---

[2] Fairburn to Geoffrey Potocki de Montalk, August 6, 1926, in Lauris Edmond, ed., *The Letters of A. R. D. Fairburn* (Auckland: Oxford University Press, 1981), p. 6.

[3] Oscar Wilde, *Soul of Man Under Socialism*, 1891.
http://wilde.thefreelibrary.com/Soul-of-Man-under-Socialism

[4] Trussell, p. 49.

having rejected Jonah and Genesis,
contrived to erect
a towering edifice of belief
on the assumption that God
is an abridgement of the calculus
and lived happily
ever after.
What is adequate suffices.[5]

ENGLAND

Potocki had left New Zealand in disgust at the cultural climate and persuaded Fairburn to join him in London, since New Zealand prevented them from doing what they were born for: "to make and to mould a New Zealand civilization," as Potocki stated it.

Fairburn arrived in London in 1930. Like Potocki, he was not impressed with bohemian society and the Bloomsbury intellectuals who were riddled with homosexuality, for which both Potocki and Fairburn had an abiding dislike.[6] Fairburn was reading and identifying with Roy Campbell's biting satire and ridicule of Bloomsbury,[7] and there was much of the "wild colonial boy" in both men's personalities.

However, away from the bohemianism, intellectualism, and pretentiousness of the city, Fairburn came to appreciate the ancestral attachment with England that was still relevant to New Zealanders through a continuing, persistent "earth-memory."[8]

---

[5] Fairburn, "The Rationalist," *Collected Poems* (Christchurch: Pegasus, 1966), p. 95.

[6] Trussell, p. 91. Throughout his life, Fairburn maintained that homosexuality was not merely a personal preference, but an actual subversion, and referred to a "Green International," an informal conspiracy of homosexuals who were distorting the arts to their own temperament. He came to regard the "dominance" of "pansies" in the arts as largely responsible for "the decadence of contemporary English and American writing." Fairburn to Eric McCormick, ca. 1951 or 1952 (Trussell, *Fairburn*, p. 249).

[7] Trussell, pp. 105–106.

[8] Fairburn, "A New Zealander at Home. Our Two Countries,"

In London, he felt the decay and decadence of the city. Like Knut Hamsun and Henry Williamson, Fairburn conceived of a future "tilling the soil." He now stated: "I'm going to be a peasant, if necessary, to keep in touch with life," and he and his future wife lived for a year in a thatch-roofed cottage in Wiltshire.

Having eschewed rationalism and godlessness early on, conceiving a land and culture in metaphysical terms gave Fairburn a deeper spirituality than he could find in modern religion, and the land became fundamental to his world-view. His reading of Spengler made him acutely aware of the land and the farmer-peasant as the foundations of a healthy culture. He was also aware of the symptoms of cultural decay and of the predominance of money-values in the "winter" cycle of a civilization, when the land becomes denuded of people and debt-ridden, with foreclosures and urban drift.

> The barn is bare of hoof and horn,
> the yard is empty of its herds;
> the thatch is grey with age and torn,
> and spattered with the dung of birds.
>
> The well is full of newts, the chain
> long broken, and the spindle cracked,
> and deep in nettles stands the wain
> three-wheeled, with rotten hay half-stacked.
>
> Where are the farmer and his bride
> who came from their honeymoon in spring
> filled full with gaudy hope and pride,
> and made the farm a good paying thing? . . .[9]

SOCIAL CREDIT

In 1931 Fairburn was introduced to A. R. Orage,[10] who had

Star, August 3, 1931, magazine section, p. 1 (Trussell, p. 91).
  [9] Fairburn, "Deserted Farmyard," *Collected Poems*, p. 89.
  [10] Trussell, p. 109.

published New Zealander Katherine Mansfield. He was also editing the *New English Weekly* which was bringing forth a new generation of talents to English literature, including Ezra Pound and T. S. Eliot. Orage was a "guild socialist," advocating a return to the medieval guilds which had upheld craftsmanship and represented interests according to one's calling rather than one's political party. Orage met C. H. Douglas in 1918 and had himself become a seminal influence on Social Credit. Orage probably introduced Fairburn to Douglas around 1931.[11]

Fairburn had read Spengler's *Decline of the West* at least as early as 1930. He saw that New Zealand, as a cultural outpost of Europe, was just as much subject to Spengler's cyclical laws of decline as the Occident.[12] It would have been with the fatalist eyes of a Spenglerian that Fairburn observed London and bohemian society and recognized in them the symptoms of decadence of which Spengler wrote, retreating to rural England where cultural health could still be found.

However, Fairburn felt that the vitality of individuals could be the answer to a reinvigorated culture, and break the cycle of decay, rather than the rise of a Caesar that Spengler stated was a kind of "last hurrah" of a Civilization before its eclipse.[13] This was despite Fairburn's earlier belief that Social Credit could only be "ushered in by a dictatorship."[14] This anti-statist, individualist belief reflects two major influences on Fairburn, that of Nietzsche and of D. H. Lawrence,[15] who espoused "heroic vitalism" as the basis of history.[16]

Spengler, however, also had much to say on the role of money and plutocracy in the final or "winter" epoch of a civilization, and of the last cultural resurgence that saw the overthrow of money by "blood," or what we might call the instinc-

---

[11] Trussell, p. 114.

[12] Trussell, pp. 109–10.

[13] Oswald Spengler, *The Decline of the West*, 2 vols. (London: Allen and Unwin, 1971), Vol. II, p. 506.

[14] Fairburn, *New English Weekly*, July 14, 1932, p. 314.

[15] Trussell, p. 113.

[16] Eric Bentley, *The Cult of the Superman* (London: Robert Hale, 1947).

tual.[17] It is not too speculative to believe that Fairburn saw Social Credit as the practical means by which money-power could be overthrown through economic reform rather than through an authoritarian "Caesar" figure. Fairburn returned to a Spenglerian theme in 1932 when writing to his communist friend, the poet R. A. K. Mason: "A civilization founded on Materialism can't last any time historically speaking of course. But it may be necessary to go through the logical end of our present trend of development before we can return to the right way of life."[18]

While Fairburn agreed with Marx that capitalism causes dehumanization, he rejected the Marxist interpretation of history as based on class war and economics. Materialistic interpretations of history were at odds with Fairburn's belief that it is the Infinite that touches man. Art is a manifestation of the eternal, of pre-existing forms. It is therefore the calling of the artist to see what is always here and bring it forth.[19]

Fairburn met the Soviet press attaché in England but concluded that the U.S.S.R. had turned to the 19th-century Western ideal of the machine. He did not want a Marxist industrial substitute for capitalist industrialism. Hence Fairburn's answer amidst a decaying civilization was the vital individual: not the alienated "individual" thrown up by capitalism, but the individual as part of the family and the soil, possessing an organic rootedness above the artificiality of both Marxism and capitalism. Culture was part of this sense of identity as a manifestation of the spiritual.[20]

Not surprisingly, Fairburn became increasingly distant from his communist friends. He was repelled by communist art based on the masses and on the fetish for science, which he called "false." He writes: "Communism kills the Self—cuts out religion and art, that is today. But religion and art ARE the only realities."[21]

---

[17] Spengler, *The Decline of The West*, Vol. II, pp. 506–507.
[18] Fairburn to Mason, January 29, 1932 (Trussell, p. 116).
[19] Fairburn to Guy Mountain, July 23, 1930 (Trussell, p. 112).
[20] Trussell, p. 111.
[21] Fairburn to Clifton Firth, December 23, 1931 (*The Letters of A. R.*

Fairburn also repudiated a universal ideal, for man lived in the particular. New Zealand had to discover its own identity rather than copying foreign ideas. Another communist friend, the photographer Clifton Firth, wrote that the "New Zealand penis was yet to be erect." To this Fairburn replied: "True, but as a born New Zealander, why don't you try to hoist it up, instead of tossing off Russia? Why steal Slav gods? Why not get some mud out of a creek and make your own?"[22]

The artist and poet William Blake appealed to Fairburn's spiritual, anti-materialist sentiments, as a means of bringing English culture out of decadence. Blake was for Fairburn "the rock on which English culture will be built in the future, when Christianity dies of an inward rot,"[23] Blake's metaphysic holding forth against the tide of industrialization and materialism.[24] Fairburn also saw in D. H. Lawrence "a better rallying point than Lenin."[25] He was similarly impressed with Yeats.[26] In 1931 he wrote to Guy Mountain that "Lawrence is the big man of the century as far as we are concerned." To Clifton Firth he wrote of a lineage of prophets against the materialist age: William Blake, Nietzsche, and Lawrence.[27] To Mason, he wrote: "our real life is PURELY spiritual. Man is not a machine."[28]

While social reform was required, it was the inner being that resisted the onrush of materialism, and Blake "was a great old boy" for what he had offered to those who fought against the material: "Social reform by all means: but the structures of the imagination are the only ones which, fortified by the spirit, can resist all the assaults of a kaleidoscopic world of matter."[29]

D. Fairburn, p. 60).

[22] Fairburn to Clifton Firth (*The Letters of A. R. D. Fairburn*, p. 60).
[23] Fairburn to Clifton Firth (*The Letters of A. R. D. Fairburn*, p. 60).
[24] Trussell, p. 113.
[25] Trussell, p. 113.
[26] Trussell, p. 114.
[27] Stuart Murray, *Never a Soul at Home: New Zealand Literary Nationalism in the 1930s* (Wellington: Victoria University Press, 1998), p. 117.
[28] Fairburn to Mason, December 28, 1931 (Trussell, p. 116).
[29] Fairburn to Mason, August 1931 (Murray, *Never a Soul at Home*,

In 1932 Fairburn wrote an article for the *New English Weekly* attacking materialism. He feared that the prosperity that would be generated by Social Credit monetary reform would cause rampant materialism devoid of a spiritual basis. He saw the aim of monetary reform as being not simply one of increasing the amount of material possessions, but as a means of achieving a higher level of culture.

Fairburn wished for a post-industrial craft and agricultural society. The policy of Social Credit would achieve greater production and increase leisure hours. This would create the climate in which culture could flourish, because culture requires sufficient leisure time beyond the daily economic grind, not simply for more production and consumption (as the declining cultural level of our own day shows, despite the increasing quantity of consumer goods available). It was the problem that Fairburn had seen admirably but impractically addressed by Oscar Wilde. However, the practical solution of it could now be sought in Social Credit, which moreover did not aim to abolish private property but to ensure its wider distribution as a means of achieving freedom rather than servitude.

In June 1932, Fairburn wrote to Mason that if the Labour Party rejected Social Credit economics,[30] he would start his own movement on returning to New Zealand:

---

p. 120).

[30] The Labour Party, mainly through the persistence of the popular John A. Lee, a one-armed ex-serviceman, was campaigning for election on a platform of nationalizing the Reserve Bank and issuing "state credit." Although this was not the same as Douglas' Social Credit, the Douglas tour of New Zealand had provided an influential impetus for financial reform. Again, at Lee's insistence, the Labour government did issue 1% state credit to finance the iconic state housing project, which reduced unemployment by 75%, but the government was too hide-bound by orthodox finance, and Lee split from Labour amidst much bitterness. See: Erik Olssen, *John A. Lee* (Dunedin: Otago University Press, 1977). Also: Cedric Firth, *State Housing in New Zealand* (Wellington: Ministry of Works, 1949) "Reserve Bank Credit," p. 7.

If I were in NZ I should try to induce Holland[31] and the Labour Party to adopt the Social Credit scheme. Then, if they turned it down, I should start a racket among the young men off my own bat. A Nationalist, anti-Communist movement, with strong curbs on the rich; anti-big-business: with the ultimate object of cutting NZ away from the Empire and making her self-supporting. That party will come in England hence, later in NZ. I should try and anticipate it a little, and prepare the ground. Objects: to cut out international trade as far as possible (hence, cut out war); to get out of the clutches of the League of Nations; to assert NZ's Nationalism, and make her as far as possible a conscious and self-contained nation on her own account. I should try, for the time being, to give the thing a strong military flavor. No pacifism, "idealism," passive resistance, or other such useless sentimentalities. Then, when the time came, a Fascist coup might be possible.

But Social Credit and Nationalism would be the main planks and the basis of the whole movement. Very reactionary, you will say. But I am quite realistic now about these things. No League of Nations, Brotherhood of Man stuff. "Man is neither a beast nor an angel": but try to make him into an angel, and you will turn him into a beast, idealism is done with — over — *passé* — gone *phut*.

Behind the labels, of course, all this would be a cunning attempt to get what we are actually all after: decent living conditions, minimum of economic tyranny, goods for all, and the least possible risk of war. Our Masters, the Bankers, would find it harder to oppose such a movement than to oppose communism. And it would be more likely to obtain support.[32]

In commenting on this, Murray stated that Social Credit drew from both the Left and the Right: T. S. Eliot and Ezra

---

[31] Harry Holland, Labour Party leader.
[32] Fairburn to Mason, June 16, 1932 (*The Letters of A. R. D. Fairburn*, p. 77).

Pound being Social Credit adherents from the Right, while New Zealand author Robin Hyde, a Leftist, also embraced Social Credit. As for Fairburn, Murray describes him as "probably one of the most notable campaigners for Douglas's ideas in New Zealand [who had] flirted with at least the theories of fascism early in the decade."[33]

On his return to New Zealand, Fairburn, instead of launching his own movement, wholeheartedly campaigned for Social Credit, mainly through his position as assistant secretary of the Auckland Farmers' Union, which had a Social Credit policy, and as editor of its paper *Farming First,* a post he held until being drafted into the army in 1943. As Trussell says of New Zealand during the early 1930s, "Everywhere now Douglas Credit was in its heyday," and in 1932 the Social Credit association was formed, followed that year by the adoption of Social Credit policy by the Auckland Farmers' Union. "Rex quickly slipped into the routine of a campaigner," speaking at Social Credit meetings, and engaging in public debates.[34]

As Trussell accurately observes, although the Social Credit association did not field candidates,[35] the victorious Labour Party incorporated some of Social Credit's "more useful concepts."[36]

NATIONAL CULTURE, ORGANIC SOCIETY

Around the closing years of the war, Fairburn began to paint in earnest and made some money as a fabric designer, necessitated by the need to provide for a wife and four children.

He spurned abstract art, and particularly Picasso, as falsifying life. Abstraction, like rationalism, was a form of intellectualism that took life apart. Fairburn believed in the total indi-

---

[33] Stuart Murray, *Never a Soul at Home,* pp. 36–37.

[34] Trussell, pp. 132–33.

[35] Orthodox "Douglas Social Crediters" do not believe in party politics, and it was therefore a contentious move when the majority of Social Crediters gradually moved into becoming a full-fledged political party, now known as the Democrats for Social Credit, a very dim shadow of what Social Credit was in Fairburn's time.

[36] Trussell, p. 135.

vidual. In art this meant synthesis, building up images, not breaking them down: "If art does anything it synthesizes, not analyses, or it is dead art. Creative imagination is the thing, all faculties of man working together towards a synthesis of personal experience resulting in fresh creation."[37]

While Fairburn believed in innovation in the arts and had earlier adhered to the Vorticist movement founded in England by Ezra Pound, Wyndham Lewis, *et al.*, he also believed that art should maintain its traditional foundations, which was a feature of Vorticism: its *classicism* was quite unique among the new forms of art arising at the time. Art is a product of an organic community, not simply the egotistical product of the artist.

Fairburn, however, saw many artists as not only separate from the community but also as destructive, calling Picasso for instance, "a bearer of still-born children," and referred to the "falseness of abstract art" and its "nihilism."[38] By way of example, Fairburn pointed to the contemporary French and Italian artists, writing of the "French Exhibition" that few of those who either scoff or praise see the art for what it is: "the great monument to industrialist and materialist civilisation."

> It is the finest expression of that civilisation that has emerged yet. But as I happen not to be a materialist, I can't accept any of the modern French painters as of any permanent importance. I'm all for Turner and the English landscape school, and for the Dutch. The Italians and the French can go and stuff themselves for all I care![39]

Fourteen years later Fairburn elaborated in a radio talk:

---

[37] Fairburn to R. A. K. Mason, December 22, 1931 (*The Letters of A. R. D. Fairburn*, p. 58).

[38] Fairburn to Firth, December 23, 1931 (*The Letters of A. R. D. Fairburn*, p. 61).

[39] Fairburn to Guy Mountain, February 4, 1932 (*The Letters of A. R. D. Fairburn*, p. 65).

Art is not the private property of artists. It belongs to the living tradition of society as a whole. And it can't exist without its public. Conversely, I think it can be said that no society can live for long in a state of civilization without a fairly widespread appreciation of the arts, that is to say, without well-organized aesthetic sensibility.[40]

Hence there was a reciprocal interaction between the artist and the public. Both possessed a shared sense of values and origins, in former times whether peasant or noble, in comparison to the formlessness of the present-day cosmopolitanism. "The artist has brought contempt upon himself by letting himself be used for ends that he knows to be destructive. By doing so he has brought art and his own type close to extinction."[41]

Geometric "form" in art is fundamental. It is the primary responsibility of art schools to teach "traditional techniques" then allow those who have genuine talent to work from there.[42]

Fairburn lectured in art history at the Elam School, Auckland University, the most influential of New Zealand's art schools which produced Colin McCahon and others. McCahon is New Zealand's most esteemed artist, whose splatters fetch millions on the market and whose influence upon new generations of artists endures. He was vehemently opposed by Fairburn, who considered his works devoid of form, "contrived," and "pretentious humbug, masquerading as homespun simplicity." "In design, in colour, in quality of line, in every normal attribute of good painting, they are completely lacking."[43]

He also considered modern music sensationalist, without content, form, or order, reflecting the chaos of the current cycle of Western civilization.[44]

Fairburn, in accordance with his nationalism, advocated a

---

[40] Fairburn, "The Arts are Acquired Tastes," radio talk; *New Zealand Listener*, July 5, 1946, pp. 21–22.

[41] Fairburn, "Notes in the Margin," *Action*, New Zealand, 1947.

[42] Fairburn, "The Auckland School of Art," *Art in New Zealand*, December-January 1944–1945, pp. 21–22.

[43] Fairburn, "Art in Canterbury," *Landfall*, March 1948, pp. 49–50.

[44] Fairburn, "Art in Canterbury," *Landfall*, pp. 49–50.

New Zealand national culture arising from the New Zealand landscape. He believed that one's connection with one's place of birth is a permanent quality, not just a matter of which place in the world one finds most pleasant to live in.

In contrast to this rootedness of being, Fairburn had early come to regard Jews as a rootless people who consequently serve as agents for the disruption of traditional society,[45] juxtaposing old England with that of the new in his 1932 poem "Landscape with Figures":

> In mortgaged precincts epicene Sir Giles,
> cold remnant of a fiery race, consorts
> with pale fox-hunting Jews with glossy smiles,
> and plays at Walton Heath, and drives a sports[46]

Writing to Mason in June 1932, Fairburn had stated that the criterion of "fortune-hunting" in choosing where one lives cannot satisfy "anybody who is un-Semitic like myself."[47] Fairburn explained to Mason that the art which is manufactured for the market by those who have no attachment to any specific place is Jewish in nature:

> The Jews are a non-territorial race, so their genius is turned to dust and ashes. Their works of art have no integrity—have had none since they left Palestine. Compare Mendelsohn and Humbert Wolfe with the Old Testament writers. When I came to England, I acted the Jew. I have no *roots* in this soil. In the end every man goes back where he belongs, if he is honest. . . . Men are *not* free. They are bound to fate by certain things, and lose their souls in escaping—if it is a permanent escape. . . . Cosmopolitan-

---

[45] Stalin came to similar conclusions from another direction, launching a campaign in 1949 against "rootless cosmopolitanism" in Soviet culture.

[46] Fairburn, "Landscape of Figures (Memories of England, 1930)," *Collected Poems*, p. 88.

[47] Fairburn to R. A. K. Mason, June 24, 1932 (*The Letters of A. R. D. Fairburn*, p. 80).

ism—Semitism—are false, have no bottom to them. Internationalism is their child—and an abortion.[48]

Fairburn condemned the notion that a culture can be chosen and attached to "like a leech" without regard to one's origins. He further identifies the impact of Jewish influence on Western culture: a contrived art that does not arise spontaneously from the unconscious mind of the artist in touch with his origins.

> Jewish standards have infected most Western art. It is possible to look on even the "self-conscious art" of Poe, Baudelaire, Mallarmé, Pater—Coleridge even—as being "Jewish" in the sense I am meaning. The orgasm is self-induced, rather than spontaneous. It has no inevitability. The effect is calculated. The ratio between the individual artist and his readers is nicely worked out prior to creation. It does not arise as an inevitable result of the artist's mental processes. William Blake, who was not Jewish, had perfect faith in his own intuitions—so his work could not fail to have universal truth—to have integrity. But the truth was not calculated . . .[49]

This cosmopolitan influence expressed an "international" or "world standard" for the arts which debased culture. He wrote: "Is poetry shortly to be graded like export mutton?"[50]

The "racket of modern art" was related to economic motives:

> . . . the infection of the market place . . . the sooty hand of commerce. The "modern art racket" has the aim of "rapid

---

[48] Fairburn to R. A. K. Mason, June 24, 1932 (*The Letters of A. R. D. Fairburn*, p. 80).

[49] Fairburn to R. A. K. Mason, June 24, 1932 (*The Letters of A. R. D. Fairburn*, pp. 80–81).

[50] Fairburn to *New Zealand Listener*, September 11, 1953 (Trussell, p. 263).

turnover," a rate of change that induces a sort of vertigo, and the exploitation of novelty as a fetish—the encouragement of the exotic and the unusual.

Fairburn's biographer Denys Trussell comments: "Rex feared that internationalism in cultural matters would reduce all depiction of human experience to a characterless gruel, relating to no real time or place because it attempted to relate to all times and places."[51] In contrast, great art arises from the traditional masculine values of a culture: "honor, chivalry, and disinterested justice."

Writing to the *NZ Listener*, Fairburn decried the development of a "one world" cosmopolitan state, which would also mean a standardized world culture that would be reduced to an international commodity:

> The aspiration towards "one world" may have something to be said for it in a political sense (even here, with massive qualifications), but in the wider field of human affairs it is likely to prove ruinous. In every country today we see either a drive (as in Russia and the USA) or a drift (as in the British Commonwealth) towards the establishment of mass culture, and the imposition of herd standards. This applies not only in industry, but also in the literature and the arts generally. In the ant-hill community towards which we are moving, art and literature will be sponsored by the State, and produced by a highly-specialized race of neuters. We have already gone some distance along this road. Literature tends more and more to be regarded as an internationally standardized commodity, like soap or benzine—something that has no particular social or geographical context. In the fully established international suburbia of the future it will be delivered by the grocer—or, more splendidly, be handled by a world-wide chain store Literary Trust . . .[52]

---

[51] Trussell, p. 263.
[52] Fairburn to the Editor, *New Zealand Listener*, June 18, 1955 (*The*

The situation today has proved Fairburn correct, with the transnational corporations defining culture in terms of international marketing, breaking down national cultures in favor of a global consumer standard. This mass global consumer culture is most readily definable with the term "American."[53]

Fairburn opposed state patronage of the arts, however, believing that this cut the artist off from the cycle of life, of family and work, making art contrived and forced instead. He also opposed the prostitution of the nation and culture to tourism, more than ever the great economic panacea for New Zealand, along with world trade. In a letter to the NZ Herald he laments the manner by which the Minister of Tourism wished to promote Maori culture as a tourist sales pitch to foreigners:

> May I suggest that there is no surer way in the long run to destroy Maori culture than to take the more colorful aspects of it and turn them into a "tourist attraction." If the elements of Maori culture are genuine and have any place outside of a museum, they will be kept alive by the Maori people themselves for their own cultural (not commercial) needs. The use of Maori songs and dances to tickle the pockets of passing strangers, and the encouragement of this sort of cheapjackery by the *pakeha* are degrading to both races. . . . And the official encouragement of Maori songs, dances, and crafts as side-shows to amuse tourists is both vulgar and harmful.[54]

This situation has since become endemic in New Zealand,

Letters of A. R. D. Fairburn, p. 228).

[53] See for example: G. Pascal Zachary, *The Global Me* (St. Leonards, New South Wales: Allen and Unwin, 2000). Zachary, a senior business correspondent, celebrates the way by which globalization is making interchangeable cogs of humanity, not bound to place or culture, to enable a more efficient utilization of talent under capitalism. The world situation seems to be precisely what Fairburn feared would develop several decades previously.

[54] Fairburn to the *New Zealand Herald*, February 4, 1955 (*The Letters of A. R. D. Fairburn*, pp. 225–26).

but where once in Fairburn's time there was the spectacle of the plastic Maori *tiki* made in Japan and sold in tourism shops, Maori culture has now been imposed as the "New Zealand culture" *per se*, as a selling point not just for tourism, but for world trade. Conversely, opening up New Zealand to the world economically has a concomitant opening up to cosmopolitanism, which usually means what is defined as "American." And the younger generations of Maori, uprooted from the rural life of Fairburn's time, have succumbed to alien pseudo-culture as conveyed by Hollywood and MTV. It is part of the "one world," "internationalized commodity standard" Fairburn saw unfolding.

In discussing the question as to whether there is any such thing as "standard English," Fairburn nonetheless affirmed his opposition to cultural standardization, including that between those of the same nationality, in favor of "personalism" and "regionalism," distinguished from "individualism," which in our own time we have seen in the form of a pervasive selfishness raised up as social, political, and economic doctrines. Fairburn writes:

> There is, first of all, the question whether it is a desirable thing for all English-speaking people to conform to a common standard in their style of speech. My own instinct leads me to resist standardisation of human behaviour in all possible contexts. I believe in 'personalism' (which is not quite the same thing as individualism), in regionalism, and in organic growth rather than mechanical order. With Kipling, I "thank God for the diversity of His creatures."[55]

A "mechanical order" pushing cultural standardization across the world is the present phase of capitalism, now called "globalization," of which Fairburn was warning immediately after the Second World War.

---

[55] Fairburn, *The Woman Problem and Other Prose* (Auckland: Blackwood and Janet Paul, 1967), "Spoken English," p. 93.

THE DOMINION OF USURY

In 1935 Fairburn completed *Dominion*, his epic poem about New Zealand.[56] Much of it is an attack upon greed and usury, and is reminiscent of Ezra Pound's *Canto XLV:* "With *Usura.*"[57]

The Labour Party's acquisition of power gave Fairburn little cause for optimism. Trussell writes that Fairburn's view was that the Labour government might introduce "a new dimension in social welfare, but apart from that he felt it to be conformist."[58]

Dominion begins by identifying the usurer as the lord of all:

The house of the governors, guarded by eunuchs,
and over the arch of the gate
these words enraged:
HE WHO IMPUGNS THE USURERS **IMPERILS THE STATE.**[59]

Those who serve the governors are picked from the enslaved, well paid for their services to "keep the records of decay" with "cold hands . . . computing our ruin on scented cuffs." For the rest of the people there is the "treadmill . . . of the grindstone god, and people look in desperation to the "shadow of a red mass" of communism"'[60] Like Pound in "With *Usura,*"[61] Fairburn saw the parasitic factor of usury as

---

[56] Fairburn, "Dominion," http://www.nzepc.auckland.ac.nz/authors/fairburn/dominionfull.asp

[57] Ezra Pound, "Canto XLV, With *Usura,*" *Selected Poems 1908–1959* (London: Faber and Faber, 1975), pp. 147–48.

[58] Trussell, p. 176.

[59] Fairburn, *Dominion*, "Utopia," I.

[60] Fairburn, *Dominion*, "Utopia," I.

[61]
> With usura, sin against nature,
> is thy bread ever more of stale rags . . .
> with no mountain of wheat, no strong flour . . .
> WITH USURA
> Wool, comes not to the market
> Sheep bringeth no grain with usura . . .

the corruptor of creativity and work, where labor becomes a necessary burden rather than a craft with a social function wider than that of profit.

> For the enslaved, the treadmill;
> the office and adoration
> of the grindstone god;
> the apotheosis of the means,
> the defiling of the end;
> the debasement of the host
> of the living; the celebration
> of the black mass that casts
> the shadow of a red mass.[62]

And . . .

> In this air the idea dies;
> or spreads like plague; emotion runs
> undamned, its limits vague,
> its flush disastrous as the rolling floods,
> the swollen river's rush; or dries
> to a thin trickle, lies
> in flat pools where swarms of flies
> clouding the stagnant brim
> breed from thick water, clustered slime.[63]

The unemployed and those on relief work, as Fairburn had been when he returned to New Zealand, were witnesses "to the constriction of life" which was necessary to maintain the financial system. Nor did the countryside escape the ravages of the system. The farms are "mortgaged in bitterness . . ." to the banks. "A load of debt for the foetus" dramatizes how the debt system of usury compounds generation after generation, with

---

> And stoppeth the spinner's cunning . . .

[62] Fairburn, *Dominion,* "Utopia," I.
[63] Fairburn, *Dominion,* "Utopia," IV.

each being placed further into serfdom to the banks, while the banker is lauded as an upstanding businessman, the new aristocrat of the age of decline that Spengler holds emerges in the "winter" cycle of Civilization. The city is:

> a paper city built on the rock of debt,
> held fast against all winds by the paperweight of debt.
> The living saddled with debt.
> A load of debt for the foetus . . .
> And all over the hand of the usurer,
> Bland angel of darkness,
> Mild and triumphant and much looked up to.[64]

Colonization had bought here the ills of the Mother Country, and debt underscored the lot:

> They divided the land,
> Some for their need,
> And some for sinless, customary greed . . .

Fairburn's answer is a return to the land.

> Fair earth, we have broken our idols:
> and after the days of fire we shall come to you for the stones of a new temple.[65]

The destruction of the usurers' economic system would result in the creation of a new order: the land freed of debt would yield the foundation for "a new temple" other than that of the usurer. Fairburn's belief in the soil as a key ingredient to cultural renewal and freedom brought him also to the cause of farmers, then allied to Social Credit.

ORGANIC FARMING

In 1940 Fairburn began to advocate organic farming, and he

---

[64] Fairburn, *Dominion*, "Utopia," IX.
[65] Fairburn, *Dominion*, "Elements," IV.

became editor of *Compost,* the magazine of the New Zealand *Humic Compost Club.* Fairburn considered that the abuse of the land led to the destruction of civilization. The type of civilization that arises depends on its type of farming, he said. Food remains the basis of civilization, but industrial farming is spiritually barren.

The type of community Fairburn sought is based on farming. Industry, by contrast, gives rise to fractured, contending economic classes. Industry reduces life to a matter of economics alone.

In a lecture to the Auckland Fabian Society in 1944 Fairburn stated:

> It is natural for men to be in close contact with the earth; and it is natural for them to satisfy their creative instincts by using their hands and brains. Husbandry, "the mother of all crafts," satisfies these two needs, and for that reason should be the basic activity in our social life — the one that gives color and character to all the rest.[66]

In the same lecture, he spells out his ideal society:

> The decentralization of the towns, the establishment of rural communities with a balanced economic life, the cooperative organization of marketing, of transport and of necessary drudgery, the controlled use of manufacturing processes . . .

In 1946 Fairburn elaborated again on his ideal of decentralization, regarding the corporation as soulless and the state as the biggest of corporations:

> The best status for men is that of independence. The small farmer, the small tradesman, the individual craftsman working on his own — these have been the mainstay

---

[66] Fairburn, "The Land of Our Life," unpublished essay, p. 5 (Trussell, p. 199).

of every stable civilization in history. The tendency for large numbers of men to forsake, or to have taken from them, their independent status, and to become hangers-on of the state, has invariably been the prelude to decay.[67]

"The broad aspect of soil politics engaged Rex's imagination: the consciousness that the fate of civilization and the shape of its culture depended ultimately on its style of farming," writes Trussell.

He hankered after a community that was itself "organic" rather than broken into a meaningless series of economic functions, and as far as he could see, the community that was founded on industrialized farming was spiritually barren even though, in the short term, it could produce huge surpluses of food.[68]

The influence of Spengler obviously remained, as did William Blake, and the aim was clearly to return through agriculture and the defeat of "Money" via Social Credit, to the "Spring" epoch of Western Civilization; an era prior to industrialization, the "City" as a Spenglerian metaphor for intellectualism and its ruler, Money, and all the other symptoms of decay analyzed by Spengler.

However utopian, Fairburn's vision was still vaguely possible in the New Zealand of his day. Today, the vision is inconceivable considering not only the rate of debt at every level of society, but due to a steady elimination of the independent farmer in favor of the corporation. If Fairburn were alive today he might well return to his original belief that such a revitalized society could only be implemented after a period of crisis, and via a dictatorship, as he had written in *The New English Weekly* in regard to Social Credit.

---

[67] Fairburn, "A Nation of Officials," in *The Woman Problem and Other Prose*, p. 47.

[68] Trussell, pp. 198–99.

NEW BARBARISM — THE U.S. & THE U.S.S.R.

Fairburn feared that the victors of the Second World War, the U.S. and the U.S.S.R., would usher in a new age of barbarism. In 1946, he wrote in an unpublished article for the *NZ Herald*:

> The next decade or two we shall see American economic power and American commercial culture extended over the whole of the non-Russian world. The earth will then be nicely partitioned between two barbarisms. . . . In my more gloomy moments I find it hard to form an opinion as to which is the greater enemy to Western civilization — Russian materialism, the open enemy, or American materialism with its more insidious influence. The trouble is that we are bound to stick by America when it comes to the point, however we may dislike certain aspects of American life. For somewhere under that Mae West exterior there is a heart that is sound and a conscience that is capable of accepting guilt.[69]

Experience has shown that Fairburn's "more gloomy moments" were the most realistic, for America triumphed and stands as the ultimate barbarian threatening to engulf all cultures with its materialism, hedonism, and commercialism. The Russian military threat was largely bogus, a convenient way of herding sundry nations into the American orbit. The U.S.S.R. is no more, while *Imperium Americana* stands supreme throughout the world, from the great cities to the dirt road towns of the Third World, where all are being remolded into the universal citizen in the manner of American tastes, habits, speech, fashions, and even humor.

Fairburn's attitude towards "Victory in Europe" seems to have been less than enthusiastic, seeing post-war Europe as a destitute, ruined, famished heap, yet one that might arise from the ashes in the spirit of Charlemagne and Jeanne d'Arc.

---

[69] Fairburn to *NZ Herald*, August 28, 1946. Trussell, p. 198.

> . . . Ten flattened centuries are heaped with rubble,
> ten thousand vultures wheel above the plain;
> honour is lost and hope is like a bubble;
> life is defeated, thought itself is pain.
>
> But the bones of Charlemagne will rise and dance,
> and the spark unquenched will kindle into flame.
> And the voices heard by the small maid of France
> will speak yet again, and give this void a Name. [70]

BIOLOGICAL IMPERATIVES

Fairburn regarded feminism as another product of cultural regression. In *The Woman Problem*[71] he calls feminism an "insidious hysterical protest" contrary to biological and social imperatives. He saw the biological urge for children as central to women.

Fairburn also considered biological factors to be more important than the sociological and economic, therefore putting him well outside the orbit of any Left-wing doctrine, which reduces history and culture into a complex of economic motives.

> Our public policies are for the most part anti-biological. Social security legislation concerns itself with the care of the aged long before it looks to the health and vitality of young mothers and their children. We spend vast sums of money on hospitals and little or nothing on gymnasia. We discourage our children from marrying at the right age, when desire is urgent, and the pelvic structure of the female has not begun to ossify; we applaud them when they spend the first ten years of their adult lives establishing a profitable cosmetic business or a legal practice devoted to the defense of safe breakers. The feminists must feel a sense of elation when they see an attractive young woman clinging to some pitiful job or other, and

---

[70] Fairburn, "Europe 1945," *Collected Poems*, p. 97.
[71] Fairburn, *The Woman Problem and Other Prose*.

drifting toward spinsterhood, an emotion that would no doubt be shared by the geo-political experts of Asia, if they were on the spot.[72]

Indeed, what has feminism shown itself to be, despite its pretensions as "progressive," other than a means of fully integrating women into the market and into production, while abortion rates soar?

It is interesting also that Fairburn makes a passing reference to the burgeoning population of Asia in comparison to New Zealand, in relation to geopolitics. The implication is that he foresaw the danger of New Zealand succumbing to Asia, which in the past few decades has indeed happened, and which proceeds with rapidity.

Fairburn saw Marxism, feminism, and Freudianism as denying the "organic nature" of man. Urbanization means the continuing devitalization of the male physically and ethically as he is pushed further into the demands of industrial and economic life. The "masculine will" requires reassertion in association with the decentralization of the cities and, "the forming of a closer link with agriculture and the more stable life of the countryside."

The influence of Spengler's philosophy can be seen in Fairburn's criticism of urbanization as leading to the disintegration of culture: "Whether this will anticipate and prevent or follow in desperation upon the breakdown of Western society is a matter that is yet to be decided."

Fairburn, along with others, especially poets such as Dennis Glover, R. A. K. Mason, Allen Curnow, and Count Potocki of Montalk, represented the great blossoming of an embryonic New Zealand culture that was starting to come into its own from out of the cultural hegemony of British colonialism. It was the type of nation-forming process that was forcefully advocated by Fairburn's contemporary "across the ditch" in Australia, Percy Stephensen.

---

[72] Fairburn, "The Woman Problem," in *The Woman Problem and Other Prose*.

The Second World War cut short what Fairburn and others had hoped to achieve: the creation of a nativist New Zealand culture. Maori culture became, as Fairburn wrote, a tourist curiosity, and the arts became just as subject to international "market forces" as any other commodity. Fairburn exposed, like no other New Zealander from the cultural milieu of the Golden Age, the forces that were bending and shaping the arts, and his polemics were a reflection of what he saw as his calling to help create a "New Zealand civilization."

Fairburn died of cancer in 1957. He continues to be recognized as a founder of New Zealand national literature—albeit one that, in this writer's opinion, was aborted and now lies fallow awaiting refertilization.

Counter-Currents/*North American New Right*
February 2, 2012

Chapter 6

Count Potocki of Montalk

"The course of my life is an indictment of the whole dishonest racket which calls itself democracy."
—Geoffrey Potocki de Montalk[1]

Geoffrey Potocki was one of the generation of the Golden Age of New Zealand literati, which included Potocki's friend and fellow poet Rex Fairburn, Allen Curnow, R. A. K. Mason, D'arcy Cresswell, and others. As one would expect, most of those who were politically inclined during this inter-war period turned to Marxism. Like Ezra Pound,[2] however, Rex Fairburn rejected Marxism in favor of Social Credit,[3] and also like Pound he even considered fascism,[4] albeit briefly.[5]

Potocki, on the other hand, turned unequivocally to the Right. Among bohemian eccentrics, he was surely the most noticeable in the London literary milieu in which he spent a significant amount of his life.

Potocki emerged from a New Zealand that was very much a British cultural outpost. Depression-era New Zealand afforded the country the opportunity to forge a sense of national and cultural identity that was something other than an imitation of Britain, while striving for its own level of excellence. Such was not to be the case, however, and what developed instead was a parochial form of Americanization, and consumer culture, par-

---

[1] Stephanie de Montalk, *Unquiet World: The Life of Count Geoffrey Potocki de Montalk* (Wellington, New Zealand: Victoria University Press, 2001), p. 19. Hereafter *Unquiet World*.

[2] *Unquiet World*, p. 84.

[3] *Unquiet World*, p. 144.

[4] *Unquiet World*, p. 86.

[5] *Unquiet World*, p. 146. Fairburn wrote to communist poet R. A. K. Mason in 1932 that if a future Labour Government did not enact a Social Credit economic policy he would start a fascist movement.

ticularly as the period following the Second World War saw the eclipse of British authority in favor of U.S. commercial banality.

Potocki, Fairburn, and even Marxists such as Mason were acutely aware of their responsibility to forge a "new civilization" in the antipodes, and some, such as Potocki in particular, self-exiled to Britain and elsewhere in the hope of finding a more fruitful cultural environment. Disgusted at the cultural climate, Potocki had left New Zealand and persuaded Fairburn to join him in London. As Potocki put it, New Zealand prevented them from doing what they were born there for, "to make and to mould a New Zealand civilization."[6]

However, in Britain, neither Fairburn nor Potocki were impressed with bohemian society, although Potocki dressed and conducted himself as an eccentric bohemian *par excellence*.[7] Nor were they impressed with the Bloomsbury intellectuals, who were riddled with homosexuality, for which both Potocki and Fairburn had an abiding dislike.

FORMATIVE YEARS

Potocki was born in Remuera, Auckland, New Zealand, on October 6, 1903. His description of his birth, related to Greig Fleming in 1993, consists mainly of astrological correspondences, showing his lifelong mystical inclination.[8] Potocki also speaks from the beginning about his own "heathenism," a problematic tendency for the claimant to the throne of Poland and Hungary, mentioning elsewhere that he "hated and despised Christian morality."[9]

Potocki, ever flamboyant, was not inclined to modesty, describing his countenance from childhood as one of great nobility which appeared "fabulous in comparison to the low level of New Zealand in that regard," one that indicated a person des-

---

[6] *Unquiet World*, p. 142.
[7] *Unquiet World*, p. 142.
[8] Greig Fleming, ed., *Aristo: Confessions of Count Geoffrey Potocki de Montalk* (Christchurch, New Zealand: Leitmotif Press, 1993), p. 15.
[9] *Aristo*, p. 30.

tined for talent and brilliance.[10]

Potocki began writing poetry at the age of eight, and decided from then that he was to be a poet.[11] Having lost his mother at an early age, and living with a step-mother who was unsympathetic, the life of Potocki and his brother became hard, including frequent starvation when his father, an architect, had financial difficulties.[12]

A Renaissance Man out of his time (a "man against time"?[13]), Potocki was fluent in French, Provencal, Latin, Greek, Polish, Hungarian, Italian, German, and Sanskrit, and in the last years of his life was learning Maori (he considered the Maori to be superior to the common run of New Zealanders).

Known for his outspokenly pro-fascist and pro-Nazi sentiments—an outspokenness not dampened by the war and life in wartime England—Potocki was, however, more than anything a traditionalist and a royalist, a neo-aristocrat who in some respects can be compared to another mystic, Julius Evola. Potocki was profoundly conscious of his identity and his lineage, and New Zealand—which prides itself on being the egalitarian society par excellence—could do nothing but repulse such a man. Potocki was to reminisce of his native land: "Life in New Zealand is a wonderful training for a future King—a superb lesson in 'How a nation ought not to be governed.'"[14]

His appearance was that of another era. In London, he sported flowing hair, a billowing cloak, large beret, and sandals. In later life, including his years back in New Zealand, he adopted the appearance of a large-bearded, robed magus, a style that during and immediately after the war was also supplemented by a self-designed "uniform" in the manner of the

---

[10] *Aristo*, p. 27.

[11] *Unquiet World*, p. 62.

[12] *Unquiet World*, p. 68.

[13] Savitri Devi, *The Lightning and the Sun* (Calcutta: Savitri Devi Mukherji, 1958), Ch. III: "Men in time, above time and against Time." Potocki's post-war friend, the avid Hitlerite Savitri Devi, formulated a cyclic paradigm of the outstanding historical individual, which was inspired by Hinduism.

[14] *Unquiet World*, p. 63.

Polish army.

Potocki's claim to Polish royal linage was legitimate enough, despite being dismissed as an "embarrassment" by his New Zealand family.[15] Count Joseph Wladislas Edmond Potocki de Montalk dispensed with his title and reduced his name down to de Montalk upon migrating to New Zealand from France in 1868, as befits a land without noble traditions other than those of the Maori.[16] The Potocki family is of ancient royal lineage, and is prominent in the history of Poland, being one of the oldest families of the nation.[17]

EARLY MUSINGS

Potocki's family moved to Nelson, in the South Island, in 1917. He did well at High School, winning a prize for excellence in English, French, Latin, and history, and was regarded by the headmaster as having a very personable character.[18] Moving to Wellington in 1918, Potocki continued to excel at school.[19] In 1919, at only 16, he became a teacher and privately studied Greek at Victoria University College. In 1921, he returned to Auckland with the aim of studying law and entered the employ of a law firm as a clerk.

By 1923 Potocki had entered the literary scene, and had met R. A. K. Mason. Despite being a newcomer, a literary group formed around him, which saw itself as a "poetic aristocracy"[20] which would revitalize English poetry. Potocki still had faith that New Zealand, as a colony, had not been infected by the decadence of the "old world." He published his first collection of poems as a four-page leaflet.

Potocki then dropped law and entered a seminary to study

---

[15] *Unquiet World*, p. 20.

[16] It is of passing interest that a few years ago, under the Helen Clark Labour government, New Zealand dispensed with the British orders of merit in favor of typically bland New Zealand orders; a decision that was reversed under the present national government.

[17] *Unquiet World*, pp. 46–47.

[18] *Unquiet World*, p. 79.

[19] *Unquiet World*, p. 79.

[20] *Unquiet World*, p. 83.

for the Anglican priesthood, not because he felt he had a divine calling but because he was attracted to the ritual and liturgy. This did not leave him in his later years, as he would attend Evensong at the Anglican Cathedral in Wellington for the same reason as he had done in his youth at the Christchurch Cathedral, despite his continued adherence to paganism. It was in seminary that he learned about missionary printing in the 19th century, and this prompted his own lifelong interest in self-publishing limited editions of his works on antiquated presses.

Potocki was briefly married in 1924. It was perhaps predictable that he could not settle down to family responsibilities. He tried to work as a milk vendor, although he could not compel himself to demand the money owed him by poor families, nor did he have an interest in money-making *per se*, surely itself a sign of innate aristocracy. He returned to Christchurch with his family and re-entered law for a short time, but continued with his real passion, poetry.[21]

In 1926 Potocki received a letter from Rex Fairburn, whom he had briefly known at primary school, and a life-long friendship ensued. Potocki assumed the role of mentor, as the more worldly-wise of the two.[22] At Easter 1927, Potocki published his first collection of poems, *Wild Oats*, which he dedicated to Fairburn.[23]

Not surprisingly, given the left-wing character of much of the literary milieu, Fairburn was flirting with communism as a means by which the artist could become economically independent to pursue his profession. However, he was not by temperament a rationalist or a materialist, and was also drawn to a spirit of aristocratic feeling that did not settle easily with socialism. Others of an artistic or literary calling who turned to the Right around the same time, men such as Ezra Pound, W. B. Yeats, and Wyndham Lewis, did so for similar reasons, fearing that a cult of the proletariat or of mass, undifferentiated

---

[21] *Unquiet World*, p. 86.

[22] Denys Trussell, *Fairburn* (Auckland: Auckland University Press, 1984), p. 48.

[23] *Unquiet World*, p. 91.

humanity, as much democratic in spirit as communistic, would result in the drowning of all real individual excellence.

Fairburn asked his royalist friend Potocki to read Oscar Wilde's *The Soul of Man Under Socialism*,[24] to show him that the aristocratic spirit and the creative genius could be accommodated under socialism.[25] However, in 1931 when Fairburn met A. R. Orage, editor of the *New English Weekly*,[26] he discovered that such freedom for creativity could not only be maintained but also enhanced by the economics of Social Credit. (Orage's magazine was from 1932 on discussing new social and political ideas, with a focus on Maj. C. H. Douglas' proposals.)[27] Fairburn had in 1930 already read and been heavily influenced by Spengler's *Decline of the West*,[28] so his rejection of Marxism was a natural development.

Fairburn was avid in promoting Social Credit and in opposing usury, whereas Potocki's perspective must be discerned from more meager sources. For example, in his pamphlet on

---

[24] As one might expect, the form of "socialism" advocated by Wilde is quite different from that pursued under Marxism. Wilde believed that socialism, or the common ownership of property and co-operation rather than competition, would free all from economic servitude and daily drudgery, and allow the creative to pursue their creativity. The "socialism" of Wilde would enhance rather than eliminate "individualism." It would not be based on the state holding economic power, as it now has political power, otherwise "Industrial Tyrannies" would result, which would be worse than the present system. Wilde saw property ownership as a "burden" and a "bore" that intruded upon one's pursuit of creativity, while lack of ownership under the present system conversely resulted in destitution. "The true perfection of man lies, not in what man has, but in what man is. . . . With the abolition of private property, then, we shall have true, beautiful, healthy Individualism. Nobody will waste his life in accumulating things, and the symbols for things. One will live. To live is the rarest thing in the world. Most people exist, that is all." http://wilde.thefreelibrary.com/Soul-of-Man-under-Socialism

[25] *Fairburn*, p. 49.
[26] *Fairburn*, p. 109.
[27] *Fairburn*, p. 115.
[28] *Fairburn*, p. 110.

New Zealand race relations written in 1987, Potocki stated: "But as far as I am concerned the present financial system busy plundering and misgoverning the world is in its higher reaches a criminal anti-human conspiracy."[29]

Stephanie de Montalk writes of the significance of Potocki and his contemporaries of this period:

> Although *Wild Oats* collected the writings of youth and, in keeping with a young man's follies, contained moments of extravagance and grandeur, it was nonetheless one of the starting points in the development of New Zealand's poetic identity. It placed Potocki among the generation of writers who would lay the basis of New Zealand literature as it developed in the 1930s.[30]

This was the Golden Age of New Zealand culture, and one which Fairburn, Potocki, Mason, Curnow, and others of the time wanted to see flourish. However, unlike what might be called the New Zealandist commitments of the rest, including Marxists such as R. A. K. Mason, and above all Potocki's protégé Fairburn, Potocki was not foremost a New Zealander but a royalist and a traditionalist.

While Fairburn and others achieved wide recognition in New Zealand, Potocki left, and only returned much later in life. He was keeping the commitment he had made to Fairburn when *Wild Oats* appeared, that his first collection was a "test" which, if it failed to gain a good response in New Zealand, would prove that the country was not fit for Potocki and he would have done with the place.[31] Potocki got mixed reviews, partly because of the bias against someone who was "in the process of dissolving his marriage." Fairburn too had had

---

[29] G. P. de Montalk, *Kahore, Kahore!* (Hamilton, New Zealand: The Mélissa Press, 1988). *Kahore* is, loosely translated, Maori for "no," or "of no benefit to us," and which Potocki states was "what the chieftains said when the *pakehas* wanted to buy Remuera."

[30] *Unquiet World*, pp. 93–94.

[31] *Unquiet World*, p. 94.

enough of New Zealand, and Potocki wrote to him that poets are treated badly there, in "this land of white savages and All Blacks" while "they are feted, laurelled and crowned in Merrie England." In October 1927, he left for England.

By 1931 Potocki was earning sufficient money to devote himself to writing, and was being published regularly back home in the Auckland and Christchurch newspapers as a feature writer.[32] It was his imprisonment in 1932 on "obscenity" charges in relation to poetry, together with his actions during the Second World War, that were to block his path to the sort of success achieved by Fairburn, Mason, and others.

By 1930, Potocki's poetic vision was already showing aristocratic and elitist traits. That same year *Surprising Songs* was published, in the foreword to which Potocki condemns "Christianity and democracy," against which he "raises the banner of the aristocratic gods, and their sons, the kings and the poets." He describes New Zealand as "Hell" from which he had fled as soon as he could. In both mystical and traditionalist tenor Potocki states that poetry is the expression of the "great spirit, the outrider of the hordes of men, the king proclaiming his kingdom, the avatar bearing in his own being a light against the darkness."[33] This and other volumes were favorably, even enthusiastically, reviewed from Europe to New Zealand.

Fairburn too now arrived from New Zealand, as disheartened by the low cultural level as Potocki, and seeing the hope of establishing a "native literature" as unlikely. However, to Potocki's disappointment, Fairburn, the quintessential New Zealander, was more interested in pub-crawls than in cathedrals.

ENGLISH LITERATI & PRISONS

At this time, Potocki was learning more about his lineage and began a tentative claim to Poland's throne, the main obstacle as he saw it being that he was not a Catholic. The claim was strengthened several years later when, in Poland, he found that the Potockis had married into the Piast family, which had

---

[32] *Unquiet World*, p. 106.
[33] *Unquiet World*, p. 110.

reigned over Poland until the mid 17th century.[34]

By now a rather well-established poet, Potocki embarked on a controversial publication that was to end his acceptance among mainstream publishers. *Here Lies John Penis* was a collection of poems, including translations from Rabelais and Verlaine, and some explicit verses in an account of some sexual misadventures by Rex Fairburn. It was intended only for distribution among friends, and was to be printed by Potocki himself on his small press.[35]

Potocki's efforts to get the type set by Leslie de Lozey resulted in the MS being taken to the police. Potocki's room was raided, and he was arrested, along with fellow New Zealand expatriate Douglas Glass.[36] Both were remanded in custody in Brixton Prison. At trial Sir Ernest Wild warned three women jurors that "this was a very filthy case indeed," two of whom excused themselves from service.

Potocki's refusal to swear on the Bible caused some consternation in court, and there was the question as to whether a pagan's oath would be acceptable. [37] The oath he swore in court was to Apollo, raising his right arm "in the Roman salute," "like Julius Caesar or Benito Mussolini," he was to later recount.[38] The verdict was "guilty." Justice Wild had not only made it very clear how the vote should proceed, he had not even allowed the jury leave to deliberate. Potocki was sentenced to six months in Wormwood Scrubs.

The case was widely reported and commented upon, generally with sympathy for Potocki. Among those who tried to help financially were W. B. Yeats, J. B. Priestly, H. G. Wells, T. S. Eliot, Bertrand Russell, Rebecca West, Aldous Huxley, and Augustus John.[39] Leonard and Virginia Woolf organized a campaign for Potocki, and questions were asked in the House of

---

[34] *Unquiet World*, pp. 120–21.
[35] *Unquiet World*, p. 131.
[36] *Unquiet World*, p. 135.
[37] *Unquiet World*, p. 146.
[38] *Unquiet World*, p. 147.
[39] *Unquiet World*, p. 160.

Commons for the case to be reviewed.[40] In the end, actual support from his well-wishers turned out to be meager.[41] The appeal heard in March 1932 was rejected.

Potocki was to relate much later to his cousin and biographer Stephanie that he believed his predicament, which ended his success as a recognized poet,[42] had actually been the result of Douglas Glass muttering unfavorable remarks about Jews in front of de Lozey when they had taken the proofs to the publisher for typesetting. Potocki had not known de Lozey was Jewish and did not understand Glass's references at the time. Potocki was informed after trial by the publisher Knott that de Lozey had taken exception to Glass's comments, and wanted him arrested, which could not be done other than by also having Potocki arrested. Potocki opined that it was really Glass that the police had been after, because he was a petty thief and a swindler.[43] These experiences in Britain left Potocki embittered towards both the justice system and the British class system. An antagonism towards Jews also emerged at that time.[44]

Some, such as the Woolfs, assumed that Potocki would go "Left," like the common run of Bloomsbury. But it is evident from his general character and outlook that Potocki was, like his contemporaries Pound, Eliot, Yeats, Roy Campbell, and others, innately and indelibly of the "Right." His royalist sympathies were manifest at an early age, and well prior to his escapades with the British Establishment.

In a chapter called "Quack, Quack" in his *Social Climbers in Bloomsbury*,[45] Potocki was to record his one meeting with the Woolfs in which Virginia sought agreement on her belief that

---

[40] *Unquiet World*, p. 158.

[41] *Unquiet World*, pp. 163–64.

[42] "I was subjected to such a boycott as is unheard of in the annals of world literature. The whole thing had a most unfortunate effect on my life. It extinguished my career as a poet." Geoffrey Potocki de Montalk, 158.

[43] *Unquiet World*, p. 177.

[44] *Unquiet World*, p. 195.

[45] Geoffrey Potocki de Montalk, "Social Climbers of Bloomsbury," *Right Review*, London, 1939.

her husband's race was much more civilized than the English and had been since ancient times. Potocki replied that, to be frank, he did not at all agree.

After his release from prison, Potocki assumed the style he was to retain throughout his life: medieval robes and a crimson cloak, modeled after the clothing of Richard II, with sandals, a velvet beret adorned with the Polish royal eagle and the Potocki coat of arms, and waist length hair that he had first allowed to grow out while in jail.

He set off for Poland in 1933, where he was welcomed by the literati and obtained employment as a translator of Polish poetry and prose into English. He was greeted with celebrity status by the press, which recognized his royal pedigree—despite the ill-informed denigration it had received from the Court in England—and remarked upon his aristocratic character and bearing.[46]

Stephanie de Montalk hypothesizes that his "anti-Semitism" might have been galvanized in Poland, having been seeded by experiences in England. However, at that time there was little need to visit Poland to draw conclusions about Jews, given on their conspicuous roles in communism and the "Left" in general. That was how Jews were widely perceived among well-informed and high-born quarters since the time of the 1917 Revolution.

Right Review

The outbreak of the Civil War in Spain in 1936 polarized the intelligentsia and literati. Some, such as Potocki and in particular Roy Campbell,[47] identified with the rebel cause. In 1935, Potocki returned to England in 1935. The following year, with funds from Aldous Huxley and Brian Guinness, Potocki bought a printing press, and began publishing his long-running literary and political journal *Right Review*. The *Right Review*, like all of de Potocki's works, was printed as limited

---

[46] *Unquiet World*, p. 207.
[47] Joseph Pearce, *Bloomsbury and Beyond: The Friends and Enemies of Roy Campbell* (London: Harper Collins, 2001), pp. 153–221.

editions but did garner the adverse attention of John Bull and the positive reaction of the reviewer for *The New English Weekly* and T. S. Eliot's *Criterion*.

Potocki's editorial in the first issue, which appeared in October, cogently describes his position:

> It is our aim to show that the Divine Right of Kings is the sanest and best form of government. . . .
>
> We are as much opposed to Capitalism, if by that term is meant Plutocracy, as any communist could be—but we are not opposed to capitalists so long as they function without damaging the interests of the whole State. . . .
>
> Neither do we consider Fascism as anything but a very bad form of government, being as it is based on demagogy, but we point out that it is a natural reaction, based on a thoroughly justifiable instinct of self-protection, whereby nations rid themselves of the socialist and communist plague. . . .[48]

Thus, Potocki's support for Fascism was critical and conditional. Fascism is a populist movement, and elitists such as Potocki were suspicious of such movements, in whatever form they took, whether Left or Right. Others of similar opinion were Evola and Wyndham Lewis.

His views on Jews did not constitute the common sort of "anti-Semitism," where Jews are generally placed in a no-win position no matter what they do. Potocki saw certain actions of many Jews as detrimental to humanity as a whole due to their own ethnocentricity and support for communism. "Aryan racialism," which presumably means Hitlerism, was therefore seen also as a "reaction" to Jewish exploits since the time of the Old Testament. Nonetheless, in disagreeing with both fascists and communists on the question of race, Potocki stated "men are to be judged by their worth as members of the human race as a whole—by their beauty, breeding, wisdom, and good will." This applies "even to Jews," but there was a duty to be

---

[48] G. P. de Montalk, *The Right Review*, No. 1, October 1936.

"very suspicious of a race" which itself "invented inhuman racialism" to the detriment of non-Jews.[49]

With the *Right Review* being published on a rudimentary press in small numbers, Potocki nonetheless started to become known among the British "Right," and he met both Sir Oswald Mosley and Mosley's propaganda chief, William Joyce,[50] the later "Lord Haw Haw" for whom Potocki's affection never wavered. Potocki seems to have retained his aristocratic suspicion of Fascist demagogy, but he did undertake printing for the British Union of Fascists.[51]

As we shall see, whatever Potocki's suspicions regarding Fascism and Hitlerism before the war, it was *after* the war that Potocki (in contrast to many others, such as Wyndham Lewis, who had supported Fascism before the war) became an avid supporter of National Socialism and Fascism. Perhaps he felt obliged to make a commitment as both a diehard rebel against the democratic *status quo*, and in realization that the post-war world was one of global democratization and Sovietization. At any rate, his sympathies after the war became more radical, rather than moderate.

The abdication of Edward VIII in 1936 was the occasion for what Potocki calls his "first political manifesto,"[52] *The Unconstitutional Crisis*. Accompanied by the writer Nigel Heseltine, who assisted with editing *Right Review*, and the artist George Hann, who provided the woodblock illustrations for Potocki's publications, they distributed large quantities of the pamphlet supporting the King in Whitehall, "at the very moment the arch-traitor Baldwin was announcing the abdication."[53] He and Heseltine were later arrested for obstruction and briefly held at Buckingham Palace. At court, Whitehall tried to intervene and have Potocki charged on the text of the pamphlet, but the judge

---

[49] G. P. de Montalk, *The Right Review*, 1936.

[50] *Unquiet World*, p. 213.

[51] *Unquiet World*, p. 213.

[52] G. P. de Montalk, *Prisoner at Buckingham Palace* (Hamilton: Mélissa Press, 1987). Reprinted in *Aristo*, pp. 53–58.

[53] *Aristo*, p. 55.

refused, and minor fines were imposed for obstruction.[54]

In 1939 Potocki set up The Right Review Bookshop in his flat, barred to "communists and racial enemies."[55] During the late 1930s he also elaborated on his pagan religious views, stating in *Whited Sepulchers* that he opposed Puritanism, Calvinism, Democracy, Christianity, and appealed to fellow pagan avengers of "the great Apostle of Paganism, Divine Julian."[56] Potocki's primary deity was Apollo and remained so throughout his life. He was by now also in the habit of greeting friends with the "Roman"—Fascist—salute, a gesture that was surely part of his rebellious nature.

KING OF POLAND

In 1939, Potocki crowned himself "Wladilsaw 5th, King of Poland, Hungary and Bohemia, Grand Duke of Lithuania, Silesia and the Ukraine, Hospodar of Moldavia, etc., etc., etc., High Priest of the Sun" in a *Rite of the Sun*.[57]

In 1940, he and his wife Odile were jailed for two months and one month, respectively, for resisting arrest, having barricaded their flat against the police, on a "black-out offence."[58] Their occupations were entered in the register as King and Queen of Poland.

Potocki's effort to register as a conscientious objector was unsuccessful, but he did succeed in evading military service. He founded the Polish Royalist Association and exchanged his robes for a military style uniform adorned with the Polish eagle and Potocki coat of arms. In the midst of war, a photograph of British Fascist leader Sir Oswald Mosley adorned Potocki's cottage in Surrey, which belonged to a member of Arnold Leese's Imperial Fascist League.

KATYN

Apart from his escapades connected to the controversy sur-

---

[54] *Aristo*, p. 57.
[55] *Aristo*, p. 57.
[56] G. P. de Montalk, *Whited Sepulchres* (London: Right Review, 1933).
[57] *Unquiet World*, p. 222.
[58] *Unquiet World*, 222–23.

rounding *Here Lies John Penis,* Potocki was most proud of being the first person in England to expose the Katyn massacre of Polish officers by the USSR. The Soviets insisted (until quite recently) that Katyn was a German war crime, and the British authorities tried to suppress knowledge to the contrary during the war lest it reflect badly on the British-Soviet alliance.

As claimant to the throne of Poland, Potocki was of course interested in Poland's future after the war. He regarded the USSR as the greatest threat to Poland's nationhood, and foresaw the likelihood of a Soviet Poland emerging from the war.[59] He put his printing skills to work for Polish exiles, which included reports that were censored in the British press. He believed that occupation by Germany was preferable to that of the USSR, despite his liking for Russians as individuals.[60] Potocki's contempt for Britain was increased by its failure to come to Poland's aid when the USSR invaded, and his support for Fascism and Hitlerism in this context became more pronounced, particularly when the USSR and Britain became allies in 1941.[61]

In 1943, hearing rumors of Soviet atrocities among the Polish community, Potocki sought the help of the Duke of Bedford, an opponent of the war and an avid proponent of banking reform, which the Duke — like Potocki[62] — saw as a major aspect

---

[59] *Unquiet World,* p. 227.
[60] *Unquiet World,* p. 228.
[61] *Unquiet World,* p. 228.
[62] Although dedicated to New Zealand race relations de Potocki mentions in *Kahore, Kahore!* that Hitler had "liberated" Germany from its "oppressors," the financiers. For the Duke of Bedford, like Potocki's friend Fairburn, the financial system was of primary concern. Bedford wrote:

> It is well to remember that the financiers of Britain and America are bitterly opposed to the Axis governments for reasons quite other than tyranny or aggression. Financiers, as has already been pointed out, desire to control the creation and issue of money in the interests of money-lending and then keep the supply short in order that people may be compelled to borrow. The Axis Gov-

of the Hitler regime, and incidentally as a cause of war. The Duke in correspondence with Potocki also alluded to the rumors he had heard about the massacre of Polish officers by the Soviet Union.[63]

In May 1943 Potocki was asked by Poles in London to expose the atrocity to the British public, and so he wrote the *Katyn Manifesto*. This was distributed by the thousands with the help of the Polish-government-in-exile. It was a "Proclamation to the English, the Poles, the Germans and the jews [sic],"[64] from the King of Poland, Hungary and Bohemia, etc. Potocki spelled out the basic facts behind Katyn and called for a negotiated peace with the hope that Germany would recognize a united Poland and Hungary, that the "jews" would be helped "if they will even at this late hour repent and behave themselves," the Tsar to be restored to Russia, and the King to France.[65]

Potocki was placed under surveillance, questions were asked in Parliament, and Potocki was attacked by the press,

---

ernments on the other hand insist on money being the servant of the State and if labour and materials are available, they order the creation of sufficient money to render possible any work which they hold to be in the national interest." (*Propaganda for Proper Geese,* p. 9, n.d., or publication details).

The pamphlet could have been written ca. 1939 when Bedford formed the British People's Party.

State credit issued at 1% interest through the Reserve Bank was also undertaken by the 1935 New Zealand Labour Government to fund the iconic State Housing project without recourse to debt. This one act eliminated 75% of unemployment; the difference with Germany here being that Labour did not have the stamina to continue to implement its election promises on banking reform. (K. R. Bolton, "The Global Debt Crisis," *Ab Aeterno,* No 3, June 2010).

[63] *Unquiet World*, p. 229.

[64] "Jews" lacked capitalization, which was to become an idiosyncrasy of Potocki's grammar also towards the "english."

[65] G. P. de Montalk, *Katyn Manifesto* (Half Moon Cottage, Bookham, Surrey, May 4, 1943). There was a *Second Katyn Manifesto* in 1983, about which more below.

including the Communist Party's *Daily Worker*, which described the manifesto as "poisonous filth,"[66] calling Potocki a "crazy Fascist Count." It was at this time that Potocki was jailed for "insufficient black-out," his wife Odile having left him for fear of his anti-government views during the war.[67] After release he was ordered by the Ministry of Labour to serve six months in an agricultural camp in Northumberland, which he attended in preference to conscription, adorned with his royal attire. After a month, he bade a "Heil Hitler" to the camp manager and left.

POST-WAR ENGLAND & PROVENCE

During another four years in England, Potocki maintained himself by printing and translations for the Polish-government-in-exile.[68] After seeking help from the Duke of Bedford for the renewal of his passport, Potocki left for France. Seeking employment at an Indian University, Potocki wrote that he had had problems with the English because of his "violently pro-Axis" outlook during the war, an attitude that would not have been necessarily offensive to an Indian given that India continues to maintain esteem (probably about equal to that held for Gandhi) for the pro-Axis Subhas Chandra Bose. He also wrote to the American Ambassador offering his services to the USA against the USSR, his naiveté concerning the USA presumably being the result of judgment clouded by his hatred of the Soviet Union.[69]

---

[66] *Unquiet World*, p. 232.

[67] *Unquiet World*, p. 234.

[68] *Unquiet World*, p. 235.

[69] It should not be assumed that being anti-Bolshevik or pro-fascist during the war made one *ipso facto* pro-USA and anti-USSR after the war. Many, unlike Potocki, Mosley, and even Evola for that matter, saw the USSR as preferable to the USA or at least as a hindrance to American cultural pathology, including such post-war "fascist" luminaries as Maj. Gen. Otto Remer, Otto Strasser, and Francis Parker Yockey. See for example: K. R. Bolton, "Yockey: 'Stalin's Fascist Advocate,'" *International Journal of Russian Studies*, Vol. 3, no. 2, June, 2010.

Potocki's pro-American attitude seems to have eventually changed

In 1949, Potocki settled in Provence, which would be his home for much of the remainder of his life, apart from sojourns in New Zealand in later years, now thoroughly "hating" the "english" (sic),[70] a word that he never seems to have capitalized. Before he was able to leave, however, the British legal system had one last go at him, charging him with assault on a female admirer after he pushed her out of his flat when she attempted to prevent his departure.

Before being fined £2, he had been assessed for several weeks at a psychiatric ward, but was found to be "perfectly healthy in every respect, both in body and mind." The authorities had expected to find a New Zealand-born claimant to the throne of Poland to be mentally unsound, but the psychiatrist was instead treated to a lucid exposition of the possibility, albeit unlikely, of Potocki becoming King on the basis that in the event of confrontation between the USA and USSR the Americans would be looking for someone who could be trusted by both Germans and Poles.[71]

Potocki settled into an old cottage in the Draguignan countryside, bought for him for £100 by the Countess de Bioncourt. Chris Martin, who knew Potocki, writes of this period:

> The Count spent his later years living in a beautiful farmhouse surrounded by olive trees in Provence. He was accompanied by a variety of lady friends and continued to work on his press. Driving around in a Citroën 2CV, flying the Polish Royal Standard he was a well-liked local figure. He also produced a translation of Adam Mickiewicz' *Dziady*, or *Forefathers*, which is the Polish national epic and the translation of which is now a standard text in a large number of American universities. The irony, if one should

---

however, as he expressed to Stephanie de Montalk his opposition to the USA anywhere in the world and the hypocrisy of condemning Germany for war crimes when the USA continued to commit such crimes in Vietnam.

[70] *Unquiet World*, p. 237.
[71] *Unquiet World*, pp. 238–40.

look for one, is that this same standard text, beautifully produced, comes with an introduction by a Jewish professor.[72] The work was—characteristically—the subject of a prolonged legal tussle between the Count and the Polish Cultural Foundation, at whose instigation the work had been translated. (It is, in passing, worth mentioning that parts of the work were recited by the translator at a concert at Leighton House, West London, together with a recital by the Count's compatriot, the pianist Richard Bielicki.)[73]

Stephanie de Montalk states that by 1958 there was a renewed interest in Potocki as part of a general interest in the literati of the 1930s and 1940s, and there was again media reportage, and his publications—mostly limited, small-run, hand-bound editions—became collectors' items, as they still are, fetching high prices.[74]

POST-WAR FASCISM

Directly after the war Potocki was not only defiantly pro-fascist but also expressed overtly pro-Nazi sympathies. His 1945 Christmas card *To Men of Goodwill* had the "X" of "Xmas" printed as a swastika, and included a six-verse poem including the words "to save his life, our William Joyce." This was at the time when Joyce, the infamous "Lord Haw Haw," was hanged for treason for his wartime broadcasts to England from Germany. It clearly shows the nature of Potocki's contempt for the era of democracy. Equally as rebellious is his 1946 four-page leaflet, *The Nuremberg Trials*, including the words "Hitler und Goering Sieg Heil."

---

[72] In reality there is no "irony," for Rightists such as Ezra Pound who also had strongly negative views about certain factions of Jewry, were not so obsessive and ignorant as to preclude the possibility of having Jewish friends and associates.

[73] Chris Martin, "'I've Spent My Life Being Me': The Life and Singular Exploits of Count Potocki de Montalk," *The Lost Club Journal*, http://freepages.pavilion.net/users/tartarus/potocki.html

[74] *Unquiet World*, p. 249.

Not surprisingly, then, it was Potocki who printed Savitri Devi's 11,000 swastika emblazoned leaflets and posters that she distributed throughout war-ravaged Germany, throwing them from the back of a train and surreptitiously posting them on walls, an action that not surprisingly resulted in her detention by the Occupation Authorities. Savitri had met Potocki in England in 1946[75] and also spent time with Potocki when she returned to London in the early 1960s.[76]

In 1959, Potocki obtained a hundred-year-old platen press and started The Mélissa Press. He now resumed his special editions, and had maintained friendships with a number of prominent literary figures, in particular Richard Aldington, who admired his efforts. Aldington wrote to Potocki that his creative work is "the only answer to the lavatory-seat wipers of literature who naturally don't recognize a poet and a gentleman when by chance they meet him."[77]

Despite his disgust at England he nonetheless commuted between Provence and Dorset, set up a press there, and issued a pamphlet advising residents of *A New Dorset Worthy*, who was "opposed to virtually every movement or line of thought triumphant at present," but that was to be expected of a "genius."[78] Among his publications was *Two Blacks Don't Make a White: Remarks about Apartheid*, published in 1964. He also printed *The National Socialist*, the journal of Colin Jordan's British National Socialist Movement.[79]

Remarks about Apartheid begins with lines from fellow Right-wing (but Catholic) poet Roy Campbell, expressing a cynicism in regard to humanitarianism as a façade for ignoble purposes: "The old grey wolf of brother love / Slinks in our track with

---

[75] Dr. R. G. Fowler, director of the Savitri Devi Archive, personal communication with the writer, July 21, 2010. Dr. Fowler states that he had interviewed two friends of Savitri who knew her when she was in England during the 1960s, and they identified the "East European Count" who printed the leaflets as Potocki.

[76] Ibid.

[77] *Unquiet World*, p. 253.

[78] *Unquiet World*, p. 265.

[79] *Unquiet World*, p. 264.

slimy fangs." Secondly, from William Blake: "One law for the lion and for the ox is oppression."

Potocki's outlook on South African Apartheid was based decidedly on the general inferiority of the blacks to whites, insofar as they had not, and could not, make a civilization. However, Potocki did not extend this white supremacy to other races, for he considered the Japanese, Chinese, and Hindus equals. In the case of white New Zealanders, he considered the Maori to be a superior race, deserving cultural and language accommodation as well as land compensation — the illiberal Potocki being far ahead of the liberals in his pro-Maori outlook.[80]

Attacks on Apartheid, Potocki claimed, were the result of the post war era of "universal humbug," the product of a coalition of Christians, communists, and democrats. He pointed to the selective hypocrisy of the liberal conscience, which was silent about communist dictatorships, and to the record of the British Empire in their treatment of colored colonials. He drew heavily on South African Government publications citing the services that had been rendered to the blacks under Apartheid, pointing out that the Afrikaners did not dispossess indigenous blacks, but had met the Xhosa while both were migrating from opposite directions. He believed that whites should react against "racial hatred" from fellow whites "whether in South Africa, Rhodesia, Smethwick or in the Deep South."[81] According to Stephanie de Montalk, the authorities in England placed an injunction against the sale of the pamphlet.[82]

In 1966, Potocki took up the cause of Rhodesia. His solution to the crisis was for "Sir Ian Smith" (sic) and the Rhodesian people to proclaim Rhodesia a Kingdom and to "offer the

---

[80] The Australian literary figure and Rightist Percy Stephensen was also of a decidedly pro-Aboriginal disposition well before it became fashionable. He helped to promote the pioneer Aborigine publication *Abo Call*, and served as secretary of the Aboriginal Citizenship Association.

[81] G. P. de Montalk, *Two Blacks Don't' Make a White: Remarks About Apartheid* (Dorset: The Melissa Press, 1964). The pamphlet is reproduced in *Aristo*, pp. 81–91.

[82] *Unquiet World*, p. 264.

Crown to His Grace the Duke of Montrose."

> In this way the Rhodesians will set the whole world a good example, take the wind out of the sails of the minority of piratical hypocrites in England, & provide a turning-point for the Good in the history of the world, at a time when it never needed it more. This would also be a piece of poetic justice, whereby the Grahams would be rewarded for their courage and loyalty during the disgraceful wars which England waged under the criminal Cromwell against Scotland and against the true interests of humanity.[83]

Potocki then outlined the genealogy of the Duke to legitimize claims to royal blood, suggesting that Rhodesia adopt the Montrose Arms as its own, which would make the country "the first of the (ex) British colonies to acquire a blazon which is a decent piece of heraldry and not an offence against good taste as e.g. the so-called coat of arms of New Zealand. . . ."

In regard to Queen Elizabeth II, Potocki declared himself to be "a pious Legitimist" and that the only lawful King of England and territories is Albrecht, "*de jure* King of Bavaria," and suggested that the Duke of Montrose might even be ahead of Elizabeth in royal succession, through Baden. Nonetheless, Potocki considered Elizabeth "an intelligent and honest girl" who should be "liberated from her servitude to her humbugging inferiors & allowed to use Her Own words as She sees fit."[84] Hence, Potocki remained as ever foremost a Royalist.

In 1977 Potocki returned to Southern African themes, namely:

> Let The Rhodesians Not
> Be surprised that England should try and sell them down the river to a gang of bolsheviks and other terror-

---

[83] G. P. de Montalk, *The King of Poland's Plan for Rhodesia* (Draguignan: The Melissa, Press, 1966).
[84] Ibid.

ists.

For after having plotted the most gigantic blood-bath and world-wide flood of misery that the world has ever seen, and carried it through by fiendish means (Dresden etc.) backed up by Hellish lies (six millions etc.) on the pretext of safeguarding the independence and territorial integrity of Poland, England shamelessly sold that great country (once the largest kingdom in Europe) to the wickedest terrorist of known history, calling himself Stalin. England has Holy Joes enough, proclaiming that "your sins will find you" — but even more surely the crimes of your country, connived at by you, will find you out. Nemesis is completely impartial.[85]

In 1987, the Count addressed New Zealand race relations, pre-empting much of what the liberals and Maori activists have subsequently sought and obtained. Potocki's plan was to restore authority to the traditional chieftains, and with the setting up of land tribunals to address grievances, to place compensated resources under the trusteeship of the Maori Sovereign. Potocki was concerned about outside interference and subversion utilizing the Maori radicals, and the likelihood of United Nations meddling in such matters or supranational law courts, which would mean that New Zealand would be "muzzled and hamstring by all the odious humbug she herself has gone in for about South Africa." Once again, he was prescient.

He regarded the Maori as having genuine grievances, which he did not accord to the Blacks in South Africa, as they had not settled that region prior to the Afrikaners, and furthermore he had an altogether higher regard for the racial qualities of the Maori than for either the Africans or for the *pakeha*.[86] He believed that a racial clash was coming, and that in the long run the *pakeha* might get the worst of things. He advocated Maori language programs and held that "they should become an in-

---

[85] G. P. de Montalk, *Let the Rhodesians Not* (Provence: The Mélissa Press, 1977).
[86] Maori term for white New Zealander.

tegral part of the social and political organization of Aotearoa." He also sought to remind New Zealanders that he was the most high-born individual who had ever been conceived in New Zealand.[87]

In the arts, he predictably saw little to praise and considered that a cultural renaissance could still be launched from New Zealand, with his assistance.[88] This optimism is surprising, since he had left New Zealand at what now transpires to have been the country's Golden Age of culture, dominated by his friends such as Rex Fairburn and R. A. K. Mason. Certainly, it reflects a degree of optimism and idealism that also accounts for it "not being impossible," given the circumstances of the post-war world, that he could have been named king of Poland.

Unsurprisingly, as part of the New Zealand literati, his cousin and biographer Stephanie de Montalk agonizes over Geoffrey's "bigotry." Yet she recalls his avid support for Maori, the genuinely warm manner with which he mingled with students of all races at Victoria University, and his enthusiastic interest in their cultures. Students for their part were impressed by his learning and his personality, Indian students by his knowledge of Sanskrit.[89]

NEW EUROPEAN ORDER

In 1969 Potocki received an "amiable invitation from the Secretary General of the *New European Order* to attend the biennial Assembly of the Order at Easter in Barcelona, as Polish delegate."[90] Potocki was skeptical, having had bad experiences with "English Fascist, semi-Fascist & pseudo-Fascist organizations," which he considered, at least among the leadership, to have been police agents and *agents provocateurs*. He was particularly scathing of Colin Jordan's' British National Socialist

---

[87] G. P. de Montalk, *Kahore, Kahore!*
[88] *Unquiet World*, p. 300.
[89] *Unquiet World*, pp. 266–67.
[90] G. P. de Montalk, *Text of a Resolution submitted to the General Assembly of the New European Order* (Draguignan, France: The Mélissa Press, 1970).

Movement, but regarded as genuine William Joyce's National Socialist League.

The New European Order had emerged as a radical faction from out of the European Social Movement, or Malmo International, founded in 1951 at the suggestion of Swedish Fascist Per Engdahl, and including support from the British Mosleyites, the Italian Social Movement, Germany's Socialist Reich Party, etc. The leaders of the New European Order were the Frenchman Ren Binet, and the Swiss Guy Amaudruz,[91] who continues to publish a bulletin of that name.

Potocki replied to the invitation by writing that his attendance was conditional on Colin Jordan not being there, and that he could propose a motion "recognizing the nullity of the Partitions of Poland (18th century) and Hungary (20th century)." The acceptance of his conditions gave Potocki "a very good opinion of the honorableness of the New European Order."[92] Potocki recounts: "I was elected enthusiastically Delegate for Poland, and my motion passed unanimously."[93] The motion reads:

> Poland and Hungary
>
> The Assembly did not believe a new order can be based on the domination of another European nation, and recognizes the invalidity of the partitions of Poland (late thirteenth century) and Hungary.
>
> The meeting considers that an understanding between the peoples directly concerned is desirable and is awaiting proposals based on the agreement of representatives of nations touched by this problem.

Potocki mentions that a few days after the congress the Croatian Delegate, General Vjekoslav Luburić, was murdered on

---

[91] Stephen Dorrill, *Black Shirt: Sir Oswald Mosley and British Fascism* (London: Penguin, 2007), p. 596.

[92] G. P. de Montalk, *Text of a Resolution submitted to the General Assembly of the New European Order.*

[93] Ibid.

what Potocki believed to have been the orders of Tito. He states that Luburić was "sincerely friendly to Poland and Hungary and spoke fluent Hungarian. PRAISE BE TO HIS NAME."[94]

Potocki also moved another resolution calling for recognition of "any human freedom" so long as it does not harm the citizen or the state, stating that some social and moral changes are irreversible and there can be no return to the 19th century. "Mindful also of a renaissance of European culture, the New European Order recognizes that 'a state of rigid disciplinary spirit could harm the development of the arts.'" The resolution deplores the political consequences of Puritanism, starting with the Cromwellian revolution. Potocki, as an advocate of aristocracy and traditional hierarchy, also considered the rebirth of high culture to be predicated on the freedom from the burden of work by the culture-bearing stratum, and the necessity of "a leisured class as useful to the culture."[95]

RETURN TO NEW ZEALAND

Potocki returned to New Zealand in late 1983, after an absence of fifty-six years, accompanied by some media interviews and commentary, and the publication of his *Recollections of My Fellow Poets*.[96] His respect among certain sections of New Zealand intelligentsia endured, however, and he was given access to an old platen press at Victoria University. Traveling to the South Island, he stopped off at Christchurch Cathedral and expressed dismay at the modernization of Anglican procedure there.

He also visited the University of Otago. The *Otago Daily Times* described Potocki as "vigorous, learned and cosmopolitan," "an avowed royalist and an enemy of democracy."

---

[94] Ibid. This is presumably Gen. Vjekoslav Luburić, commander of the Ustase concentration camps in Croatia during World War II. After the war, he was active in Croatian emigrant communities and founded the underground Croatian National Resistance. As Potocki insisted, Luburich was killed by an agent of UDBA, the Yugoslav secret service, Ilija Stanich, on April 20, 1969, in Carcaixent, Spain.
[95] Ibid.
[96] *Unquiet World*, p. 122.

Potocki was reported as stating: "The whole thesis upon which democracy is based is totally unjust . . . like one man, one vote. The biggest idiot can have a vote whereas a valuable person also has one vote." The undimming of his aristocratic views in the aftermath of the victory of democracy might be accounted for by the *Times* comment that, "he said he did not care about public opinion because the public were stupid."[97] With such views, it is clear enough why he had not been in New Zealand, the epitome of democratic and egalitarian values, for 56 years, "where no creative life exists except in animal form, and where all the loveliness of European civilization exists only in a weird state of caricature."[98] An interesting and worthy account of his life was produced and aired on the *Tuesday Documentary* of Television One in 1984, entitled *The Count – Profile of a Polemicist*.

Spending the summer in Provence in 1985, he returned to New Zealand later that year, and moved into a friend's house in Hamilton, a city of loathsome pseudo-academics and charlatans with an equally loathsome university administration.

Dr. F. W. Nielsen Wright, an energetic poet, critic, and chronicler of New Zealand culture, describes Potocki as "the all time bad boy of Aotearoa letters."[99] Wright, a notable figure in New Zealand literature, and former professor of English at Victoria University, also involved in the obscure and short-lived Communist Party of Aotearoa, states that "nobody else comes close to Potocki," and that he was "treated as a pariah by New Zealand academics[100] without exception to the day of his death."

Potocki should long ago have been awarded a Doctorate

---

[97] *Unquiet World*, p. 127.

[98] *Unquiet World*, p. 153.

[99] F. W. Nielsen Wright, *Count Potocki de Montalk: the all time bad boy of Aotearoa letters, news of some recent developments in Potocki studies*, (Wellington, New Zealand: Cultural and Political Booklets, Monograph of Aotearoa literature No. 12, 1997), p. 3. As Wright explains, both he and Potocki preferred the Maori name for New Zealand.

[100] Given the troglodyte nature of New Zealand academe in the social sciences this pariah status is surely an honor.

of Letters for his translation into verse . . . of the Polish classic, *Forefather's Eve*, a romantic verse play by Adam Mickiewicz. This translation has a higher standing internationally than any other piece of New Zealand verse.[101]

In 1990, Potocki travelled to Poland at the invitation of Dr. Andrzej Klossowski of Warsaw University and the Polish National Library and gave well-attended readings of his poetry.[102] In 1993 Fleming's collection of interviews and writings by Potocki was launched. That same year, Potocki returned to Provence despite declining health.

Potocki died on April 14, 1997 at Draguignan. His grave was marked by a simple granite slab etched "G. Potocki de Montalk 1903–1997."[103]

Wright states that on Potocki's death in France of "extreme old age" his personal papers were shipped back to New Zealand. This caused protest from the French Government which regarded them as a French cultural treasure. To Wright it was Potocki who was

> . . . the leading figure in a group of Aotearoa writers who in the 1920s asserted the value of poetry and challenged their fellow countrymen and women to give them recognition and honor as poets. . . . All felt that the country in fact rejected them and all went into external or internal exile. But their claim remains true. They are the most outstanding group of poets so far in our literature in English.
>
> He has never been forgiven in New Zealand for espousing fascism, even though other literary figures who went the same way have long since been rehabilitated and count as honored writers: people like Knut Hamsun in Norway, Maurras in France, Ezra Pound in the United States, and P. G. Wodehouse in Britain.[104]

---

[101] *Count Potocki de Montalk.*
[102] *Count Potocki de Montalk*, p. 302.
[103] *Count Potocki de Montalk*, p. 316.
[104] *Count Potocki de Montalk*, pp. 4–5.

"A Good European"

In pondering the Count's character, Chris Martin wrote:

How best to describe the Count? Whilst possessed of opinions with which I personally often disagreed, he was a small and handsome figure, extremely attractive to the ladies, exceptionally well-spoken (to the extent of correcting my own English), obviously extremely talented but, equally obviously, an embittered victim of the English judicial system, and what in 1932 passed for reality. His nephew Peter Potocki described him as "Uncle Nero." I can state personally that the Count was an extremely interesting person to know; his position in literary history is pretty well irrefragable. However, I will say that he was most interesting company and one of the most informed people one has met about virtually any aspect of European history. For a person born in New Zealand in 1903, the Count was what, with Nietzsche, we might term "a good European."

Counter-Currents/*North American New Right*
August 14–16, 2010

CHAPTER 7

YUKIO MISHIMA

Yukio Mishima (1945–1970) was born into an upper middle-class family. Novelist, essayist, playwright, and actor, he has been described as the "Leonardo da Vinci of contemporary Japan,"[1] and is one of the few Japanese writers to have become widely known and translated in the West.

THE DARK SIDE OF THE SUN
Since World War II, the West has forgotten what C. G. Jung would have termed the "Shadow" soul of Japan, the collective impulses that have been repressed by the "Occupation Law" and the imposition of democracy. The Japanese are seen stereotypically as being overly polite and smiling business executives and camera snapping tourists. The soft counterpart of the Japanese psyche, the "chrysanthemum" (the arts), has been emphasized, while the "sword" (the martial tradition) has been repressed.[2]

The American cultural anthropologist Ruth Benedict wrote of the duality of the Japanese character using this symbolism in her study, *The Chrysanthemum and the Sword*,[3] to which Mishima referred approvingly.[4] Benedict had been commissioned by the US government in 1944 to write a study of Japanese culture. Portraying the Japanese as savages was fine for the purpose of war propaganda, but a more nuanced understanding was considered necessary for post-war dealings.

What Benedict described was the ethos of probably every Traditional society, regardless of time, place, and ethnicity.

---

[1] Henry Scott Stokes, *The Life and Death of Yukio Mishima* (Harmondsworth: Penguin Books, 1985), p. 15.

[2] Stokes, p. 18.

[3] Ruth Benedict, *The Chrysanthemum and the Sword*, 1946 (New York: Mariner Books, 2005).

[4] Stokes, p. 18.

This "perennial Tradition" was described by Julius Evola, who showed that traditional cultures have analogous outlooks. They perceive the earthly as a reflection of the cosmos, the mortal as a reflection of the divine. They regard the King or Emperor as a link between the earth and the cosmos, the human and the divine. This was the Traditionalist ethos W. B. Yeats desired to revive in Western Civilization, in a manner similar to Mishima's demand for the revival of the Samurai ethic in Japan. In such traditional societies, the King is also a priest who serves as the direct link to the divine,[5] the warrior is honored rather than the merchant, and society is strictly hierarchical and regarded as an earthly reflection of divine order. Fulfilling one's divinely-ordained duty as a king, soldier, priest, peasant, or merchant is the purpose of each individual's life, and is sanctioned by law and religion.

Hence, in traditional societies the role of the merchant is subordinate, and the rule of money — *plutocracy* — as in the West today, is regarded as an inversion of the traditional ethos, a symptom of cultural decay. In traditional Japan, as Inazo Nitobe explains:

> Of all the great occupations in life, none was further removed from the profession of arms than commerce. The merchant was placed lowest in the category of vocations — the knight, the tiller of the soil, the mechanic, the merchant. The samurai derived his income from the land and could even indulge, if he had a mind to, in amateur farming; but the counter and abacus were abhorred.[6]

---

[5] Evola states of this: "Every traditional civilization is characterized by the presence of beings who, by virtue of their innate or acquired superiority over the human condition, embody within the temporal order the living and efficacious presence of a power that comes from above." Hence, the Roman *Pontifex* for example, means "a builder of bridges" between the natural and the supernatural. Julius Evola, *Revolt Against the Modern World* (Rochester, Vermont: Inner Traditions International, 1995), p. 7.

[6] Inazo Nitobe, *Bushido: The Code of the Samurai*, 1899 (Sweetwater Press, 2006), p. 104.

Nitobe states that when Japan opened up to foreign commerce, feudalism was abolished, the Samurai's fiefs were taken, and he was compensated with bonds, with the right to invest in commerce. Hence the Samurai was degraded to the status of a merchant in order to survive.[7]

According to Benedict, during the war, the Japanese regarded themselves as the only nation left in the world that had maintained the divine order. They believed it their duty to reimpose this order upon the rest of the world. Japan's *Bushido*, the "Way of the Knight," is therefore analogous to that of other traditionalist societies, such as the chivalry of Medieval Europe and the warrior code explained by Krishna to Arjuna in the Bhagavad Gita. To the Japanese warrior aristocracy the sword (*katana*) was a sacred object, forged with ceremony, its use subject to precise rules.[8]

Mishima insisted that Japan return to a balance of the arts and the martial spirit. To use, once again, the terminology of Jung, Mishima was calling Japan to "individuation" by allowing the repressed "Shadow" archetype, "The Sword," to reassert itself. Mishima was himself a synthesis of scholar and warrior who rejected pure intellectualism and theory in favor of action.

Nitobe, in explaining *Bushido*, wrote that intellectualism was looked down upon by the Samurai. Learning was valued not as an intellectual exercise but as a matter of character formation. Intellect was considered subordinate to ethos. Man and the universe were both spiritual and ethical. The cosmos had a moral imperative.[9] This was discussed by Mishima in his commentary on *Hagakure*.

The American occupation was such an inversion of the Japanese spirit that Ian Buruma, writing in the "Foreword" to the 2005 edition of *The Chrysanthemum and the Sword*, states:

> Young Japanese today might have a hard time recognizing

---

[7] Nitobe, p. 105.
[8] Evola, p. 84.
[9] Nitobe, p. 59.

some aspects of the "national character" described in Benedict's book. Loyalty to the Emperor, duty to one's parents, terror of not repaying one's moral debts, these have faded in an age of technology-driven self-absorption.[10]

THE WAY OF THE SAMURAI

Mishima's aesthetic ideal was the beauty of a violent death in one's prime, an ideal common in classical Japanese literature. As a sickly youngster, Mishima's ideal of the heroic death had already taken hold: "A sensuous craving for such things as the destiny of soldiers, the tragic nature of their calling . . . the ways they would die."[11]

He was determined to overcome his physical weaknesses. There is much of the Nietzschean "Higher Man" about him, of overcoming personal and social restraints to express his own heroic individuality.[12] His motto was: "Be Strong."[13]

The Second World War had a formative influence on Mishima. Along with his fellow students, he felt that conscription and certain death awaited.[14] He became chairman of the college literary club, and his patriotic poems were published in the student magazine.[15] He also co-founded his own journal and began to read the Japanese classics, becoming associated with the nationalistic literary group *Bungei Bu*, who believed war to be holy.

However, Mishima barely passed the medical examination for military training. He was drafted into an aircraft factory where *kamikaze* planes were manufactured.[16]

In 1944, he had his first book, *Hanazakan no Mori* (*The Forest in Full Bloom*) published,[17] a considerable feat in the final year of the war, which brought him instant recognition.

---

[10] Ian Buruma, Foreword, *The Chrysanthemum and the Sword*, p. xii.
[11] Mishima, *Confessions of a Mask* (London: Peter Owen, 1960), p. 14.
[12] Mishima was "well versed in Nietzsche" (Stokes, p. 152).
[13] Stokes, p. 72.
[14] Stokes, p. 80.
[15] Stokes, p. 81.
[16] Stokes, p. 89.
[17] Stokes, p. 89.

While Mishima's role in the war effort was obviously not as he would have wished, he spent the rest of his life in the postwar world attempting to fulfill his ideals of Tradition and the Samurai ethic, seeking to return Japan to what he regarded as its true character amidst the democratic era in which the ideal of "peace" is an unquestioned absolute (even though it has to be continually enforced with much military spending and localized wars).

THE WILL TO HEALTH

In 1952, Mishima, then an established literary figure, traveled to the USA. Sitting in the sun aboard ship, something he had been unable to do in his youth because of his weak lungs, Mishima resolved to match the development of his physique with that of his intellect.

His interest in the Hellenic classics took him to Greece. He wrote that, "In Greece there had been however an equilibrium between the physical body and intelligence, *soma* and *sophia* . . ." He discovered a "Will towards Health," an adaptation of Nietzsche's "Will to Power," and he was to become almost as noted as a body builder as he was a writer.[18]

LITERARY ASSAULT

In 1966, Mishima wrote: "The goal of my life was to acquire all the various attributes of the warrior."[19] His ethos was that of the Samurai *Bunburyodo-ryodo*: the way of literature (*Bun*) and the Sword (*Bu*), which he sought to cultivate in equal measure, a blend of "art and action."[20] "But my heart's yearning towards Death and Night and Blood would not be denied." His ill-health as a youth had robbed him of what he clearly viewed as his true destiny: to have died during the War in the service of the Emperor, like so many other young Japanese. He expressed the Samurai ethos:

---

[18] Stokes, p. 119.
[19] Stokes, p. 152.
[20] Mishima, *Sun and Steel* (London: Kodansha International, 1970), p. 49.

To keep death in mind from day to day, to focus each moment upon, inevitable death . . . the beautiful death that had earlier eluded me[21] had also become possible. I was beginning to dream of my capabilities as a fighting man.[22]

In 1966, Mishima applied for permission to train at army camps and the following year wrote *Runaway Horses*, the plot of which involves Isao, a radical Rightist student and martial arts practitioner, who commits *hara-kiri* after fatally stabbing a businessman. Isao had been inspired by the book *Shinpuren Shiwa* ("The History of Shinpuren") which recounts the Shinpuren Incident of 1877, the last stand of the Samurai when, armed only with spears and swords, they attacked an army barracks in defiance of government decrees prohibiting the carrying of swords in public and ordering the cutting off of the Samurai topknots. All but one of the Samurai survivors committed *hara-kiri*. Again Mishima was using literature to plot out how he envisaged his own life unfolding, and ending, against the backdrop of tradition and history.

In 1960 Mishima wrote the short story "Patriotism," in honor of the 1936 *Ni ni Roku* rebellion of army officers of the *Kodo-ha* faction who wished to strike at the Soviet Union in opposition to the rival *Tosei-ha*, who aimed to strike at Britain and other colonial powers.

The 1936 rebellion impressed itself on Mishima, as had the suicidal but symbolic defiance of the last Samurai in the Shinpuren Incident of 1877. In "Patriotism" the hero, a young officer, commits *hara-kiri*, of which Mishima states: "It would be difficult to imagine a more heroic sight than that of the lieutenant at this moment."[23]

Mishima again wrote of the incident in his play *Toka no Kiku*[24] Here he criticizes the Emperor for betraying the *Kodo-ha*

---

[21] During World War II.
[22] Mishima, *Sun and Steel*, p. 59.
[23] Mishima, "Patriotism," *Death in Midsummer and Other Stories* (New Directions, 1966), p. 115.
[24] Stokes comments that Mishima "was a brilliant playwright, per-

officers and for renouncing his divinity after the war, which Mishima viewed as a betrayal of the war dead. Mishima combined these three works on the rebellion into a single volume called the *Ni ni Roku* trilogy.

Mishima comments on the Trilogy and the rebellion:

> Surely some God died when the *Ni ni Roku* incident failed. I was only eleven at the time and felt little of it. But when the war ended, when I was twenty, a most sensitive age, I felt something of the terrible cruelty of the death of that God . . . the positive picture was my boyhood impression of the heroism of the rebel officers. Their purity, bravery, youth and death qualified them as mythical heroes; and their failures and deaths made them true heroes in this world . . .[25]

Mishima frequently expresses the sentiment that "failure and death" — the outcomes of both the 1877 and 1936 rebellions — made the traditionalist rebels "true heroes in this world." This indicates that Mishima regarded not the result of an action as of significance but the purity of the action *per se*. This attitude goes beyond politics, which aims to achieve results, or "the art of the possible," and enters the realm of what the Hindu would call *dharma*.

In early 1966, Mishima systemized his thoughts in an 80-page essay entitled *Eirei no Koe*,[26] again based on the *Ni ni Roku* rebellion. In this work he asks, "why did the Emperor have to become a human being?"[27] While the work remained obscure, it provided the basis for the founding of his paramilitary Shield Society two years later.

In a 1966 interview with a Japanese magazine, Mishima upheld the imperial system as the only type suitable for Japan. All

---

haps the best playwright of the post-war era in Japan. His dialogue was superb and the structure of his plays excellent." (p. 170).

[25] Mishima, cited by Stokes, p. 200.

[26] Mishima, *The Voices of the Heroic Dead,* 1966.

[27] Stokes, p. 200.

the moral confusion of the post-war era, he states, stems from the Emperor's renunciation of his divine status. The move away from feudalism to capitalism and the consequent industrialization disrupts the relationships between individuals. Real love between a couple requires a third term, the apex of a triangle embodied in the divinity of the Emperor.[28]

THE TATENOKAI

In 1968 Mishima created his own militia, the *Tatenokai* (Shield Society) writing shortly before of reviving the "soul of the Samurai within myself." Permission was granted by the army for Mishima to use their training camps for the student followers he recruited from several Right-wing university societies.

At the office of a Right-wing student journal, a dozen youths gathered. Mishima wrote on a piece of paper: "We hereby swear to be the foundation of *Kokoku Nippon*."[29] He cut a finger, and everyone else followed, letting the blood fill a cup. Each signed the paper with their blood and drank from the cup. The *Tatenokai* was born.[30]

The principles of the society were:

1. Communism is incompatible with Japanese tradition, culture, and history and runs counter to the Emperor system;
2. The Emperor is the sole symbol of our historical and cultural community and racial identity; and
3. The use of violence is justifiable in view of the threat posed by communism.[31]

The militia was designed to have no more than 100 members, and to be a "stand-by" army concentrating only on training, without any political agitation. The metaphysical basis of Mi-

---

[28] *Sunday Mainichi*, March 8, 1966.
[29] "Imperial Japan."
[30] Stokes, p. 203.
[31] Stokes, p. 205.

shima's thinking for the militia was expressed by his description of the *Tatenokai* as "the world's least armed, most spiritual army."[32] They were following the path of tradition, which had sustained the Japanese during World War II against overwhelming *material* forces, as described by Ruth Benedict.[33] Mishima referred to Benedict's book when explaining that his reason for creating the *Tatenokai* was to restore to Japan the balance of the "chrysanthemum and the sword" which had been lost after the war.[34] The emblem that Mishima designed for the society comprised two ancient Japanese helmets in red against a white silk background.

By this time, Mishima felt that his calling as a novelist was completed. It must have seemed the right time to die. He had been awarded the Shinchosha Literary Prize in 1954 for *The Sound of Waves* and the Yomiuri Literary Prize in 1957 for *The Temple of the Golden Pavilion*. His novels *Spring Snow* and *Runaway Horses* had sold well, but he was aggravating the literati, amongst whom his sole defender at this time was Yasunari Kawabata, who had received the Nobel Prize for Literature in 1968. (Mishima missed out because the Nobel Prize committee assumed he could wait awhile longer in favor of his mentor.) Kawabata considered Mishima's literary talent to be exceptional.

Mishima characterized the intelligentsia as ". . . the strongest enemy within the nation. It is astonishing how little the character of modern intellectuals in Japan has changed, i.e., their cowardice, sneering, 'objectivity,' rootlessness, dishonesty, flunkeyism, mock gestures of resistance, self-importance, inactivity, talkativeness, and readiness to eat their words."

HAGAKURE

Mishima's destiny was shaped by the Samurai code expounded in a book he had kept with him since the war. This was *Hagakure*, the best-known line of which is: "I have discov-

---

[32] *Queen Magazine*, England, January 1970.
[33] Benedict, p. 21. See below.
[34] Comments to Stokes, p. 227.

ered that the way of the Samurai is death."

Hagakure was the work of the 17th-century Samurai Jocho Yamamoto, who dictated his teachings to his student Tashiro. *Hagakure* became the moral code taught to the Samurai, but did not become available to the general public until the latter half of the 19th century. During World War II it was widely read, and its slogan on the way of death was used to inspire the *Kamikaze* pilots. Following the Occupation it went underground, and many copies were destroyed lest they fall into American hands.[35]

Mishima wrote his own commentary on *Hagakure* in 1967.[36] He stated in his introduction that it was the one book he referred to continually in the 20 years since the war and that during the war he had always kept it close to him.[37]

Mishima relates that immediately following the war, he felt isolated from the rest of literary society, which had accepted ideas that were alien to him. He asked himself what his guiding principle would be now that Japan was defeated. *Hagakure* was the answer, providing him with "constant spiritual guidance" and "the basis of my morality." Like all other Japanese books of the war period, *Hagakure* had become loathsome in the democratic era, to be purged from memory. But Mishima found that in the darkness of the times it now radiated its "true light."[38]

> It is now that what I had recognized during the war in *Hagakure* began to manifest its true meaning. Here was a book that preached freedom, that taught passion. Those who have read carefully only the most famous line from *Hagakure* still retain an image of it as a book of odious fanaticism. In that one line, "I found that the Way of the

---

[35] Kathryn Sparling, "Translator's Note," *Yukio Mishima on Hagakure: The Samurai Ethic and Modern Japan*, 1967 (New York: Basic Books, 1977), p. viii.

[36] *Yukio Mishima on Hagakure: The Samurai Ethic and Modern Japan*, 1967 (New York: Basic Books, 1977).

[37] *Mishima on Hagakure*, p. 4.

[38] *Mishima on Hagakure*, pp. 5–6.

Samurai is death," may be seen the paradox that symbolizes the book as a whole. It was this sentence, however, that gave me the strength to live.[39]

THE FEMINIZATION OF SOCIETY

One of the primary themes of interest for the present-day Western reader of Mishima's commentary on *Hagakure* is his use of Jocho's observations on his own epoch to analyze the modern era. Both 17th-century Japan and 20th-century Japan manifest analogous symptoms of decadence, the latter due to the imposition of alien values that are products of the West's cycle of decay, while those of Jocho's day indicate that Japanese civilization in his time was also in a phase of decay. Therefore, those interested in cultural morphology, Spengler's in particular, will see analogues to the present decline of Western civilization in Jocho's analysis of his time and Mishima's analysis of post-war Japan.

The first symptom considered by Mishima is the obsession of youth with fashion. Jocho observed that even among the Samurai, the young talked only of money, clothes, and sex, an obsession that Mishima observed in his time as well.[40]

Mishima also pointed out that the post-war feminization of the Japanese male was noted by Jocho during the peaceful years of the Tokugawa era. Eighteenth-century prints of couples hardly distinguish between male and female, with similar hairstyles, clothes, and facial expressions, which make it almost impossible to tell which is which. Jocho records in *Hagakure* that during his time, the pulse rates of men and women, which usually differ, had become the same, and this was noted when treating medical ailments. He called this "the female pulse."[41] Jocho observed: "The world is indeed entering a degenerate stage; men are losing their virility and are becoming just like women..."

---

[39] *Mishima on Hagakure*, p. 6.
[40] *Mishima on Hagakure*, p. 17. Jocho, *Hagakure*, Book One.
[41] *Mishima on Hagakure*, pp. 18–19. Jocho, *Hagakure*, Book One.

CELEBRITIES REPLACE HEROES

Jocho condemns the idolization of certain individuals achieving what we'd today call celebrity status. Mishima comments:

> Today, baseball players and television stars are lionized. Those who specialize in skills that will fascinate an audience tend to abandon their existence as total human personalities and be reduced to a kind of skilled puppet. This tendency reflects the ideals of our time. On this point there is no difference between performers and technicians.
>
> The present is the age of technocracy (under the leadership of technicians); differently expressed, it is the age of performing artists. . . . They forget the ideals for a total human being; to degenerate into a single cog, a single function becomes their greatest ambition . . .[42]

The spectacle of Hollywood and everything that the words "star" and "celebrity" suggest epitomize the cultural banality of the world today.

THE BOREDOM OF PACIFISM

Under pacifism and democracy, the individual is literally dying of boredom, rather than living and dying heroically: "Ours is an age in which everything is based on the premise that it is best to live as long as possible. The average life span has become the longest in history, and a monotonous plan for humanity unrolls before us."[43]

Once a young man finds his place in society, his struggle is over, and there is nothing left for youth apart from retirement, "and the peaceful, boring life of impotent old age." The comfort of the welfare state ensures against the need to struggle, and one is simply ordered to "rest." Mishima comments on the extraordinary number of elderly who commit suicide.[44] Now we might add the even more extraordinary number of youth

---

[42] *Mishima on Hagakure*, pp. 20–21.
[43] *Mishima on Hagakure*, p. 24.
[44] *Mishima on Hagakure*, pp. 24–25.

who commit suicide.

Mishima equates socialism and the welfare state, and finds that at the end of the first, there is "the fatigue of boredom" while at the end of the second there is suppression of freedom. People desire something to die for, rather than the endless peace that is upheld as utopia. Struggle is the essence of life. To the Samurai, death is the focus of life, even in times of peace. "The premise of the democratic age is that it is best to live as long as possible."[45]

The Repression of Death

The modern world seeks to avoid the thought of death. Yet the repression of such a vital element of life, like all such repressions, will lead to an ever-increasing explosive tension. Mishima states:

> We are ignoring the fact that bringing death to the level of consciousness is an important element of mental health . . . *Hagakure* insists that to ponder death daily is to concentrate daily on life. When we do our work thinking that we may die today, we cannot help feeling that our job suddenly becomes radiant with life and meaning.[46]

Extremism

Mishima states that *Hagakure* is a "philosophy of extremism." Hence, it is inherently out of character in a democratic society. Jocho stated that while the Golden Mean is greatly valued, for the Samurai one's daily life must be of a heroic, vigorous nature, to excel and to surpass. Mishima comments that "going to excess is an important spiritual springboard."[47]

Intellectualism

Mishima held intellectuals in the same contempt as Westerners also in revolt against the modern world, such as D. H. Lawrence, who believed that the life force is repressed by ra-

---

[45] *Mishima on Hagakure*, p. 27.
[46] *Mishima on Hagakure*, p. 29.
[47] *Mishima on Hagakure*, p. 61.

tionalism and intellectualism and replaced by the counting house mentality of the merchant, not just in business but in all aspects of life. Jocho stated that:

> The calculating man is a coward. I say this because calculations have to do with profit and loss, and such a person is therefore preoccupied with profit and loss. To die is a loss, to live is a gain, and so one decides not to die. Therefore one is a coward. Similarly a man of education camouflages with his intellect and eloquence the cowardice or greed that is his true nature. Many people do not realise this.[48]

Mishima comments that in Jocho's time there was probably nothing corresponding to the modern intelligentsia. However, there were scholars, and even the Samurai themselves had begun to form into a similar class "in an age of extended peace." Mishima identifies this intellectualism with "humanism," as did Spengler. This intellectualism means, contrary to the Samurai ethic, that "one does not offer oneself up bravely in the face of danger."[49]

NO WORDS OF WEAKNESS

The Samurai in times of peace still talks with a martial spirit. Jocho taught that, "the first thing a Samurai says on any occasion is extremely important. He displays with this one remark all the valor of the Samurai."[50] Jocho stated: "Even in casual conversation, a Samurai must never complain. He must constantly be on his guard lest he should let slip a word of weakness." "One must not lose heart in misfortune."

THE FLOW OF TIME

Jocho's reference to "the flow of time" indicates that he recognized the cyclic nature of the life of a cultural organism four

---

[48] *Mishima on Hagakure*, p. 67. Jocho (Book One).
[49] *Mishima on Hagakure*, p. 69.
[50] *Mishima on Hagakure*, p. 74. Jocho (Book One).

hundred years before Spengler explained it to the West.[51] Mishima points out that while Jocho laments "the decadence of his era and the degeneration of the young Samurai," he observes "the flow of time," realistically stating that it is no use resisting that flow.[52] As Jocho stated: "The climate of an age is unalterable. That conditions are worsening steadily is proof that we have entered the last stage of the Law."[53]

Jocho employs the analogy of seasons just as Spengler did in describing the cycles of a civilization: "However, the season cannot always be spring or summer, nor can we have daylight forever. What is important is to make each era as good as it can be according to its nature."[54] Jocho does not recommend either nostalgia for the return of the past, or the "superficial" attitude of those who only value what is modern, or "progressive" as we call it today.

A SAMURAI'S DESTINY

Mishima's literary output was like his own personal military plan of attack upon the modern era, in keeping with the Way of the Samurai. Mishima would not have expected a final act of defiance against the modern world to end in "victory" in any conventional sense. Having been imbued with the traditional ethos of Japan during the war, it was the spiritual dimension that mattered. Against vastly superior material forces, this spiritual dimension had sustained Japan's "mission" to bring hierarchy to the East and to the Pacific, as the only nation that had maintained this traditionalist outlook. Benedict records that this belief was retained in the immediate post-war era and that this was still motivated by a spiritual outlook:

> Japan likewise put her hopes of victory on a different

---

[51] Oswald Spengler, *The Decline of The West* (London, George Allen and Unwin, 1971).

[52] *Mishima on Hagakure*, p. 82.

[53] This refers to the entering of three progressively degenerate stages according to the Buddhist cycles of history. *Mishima on Hagakure*, p. 95, note 11.

[54] *Mishima on Hagakure*, p. 83.

basis from that prevalent in the United States. She would win, she cried, a victory of spirit over matter. America was big, her armaments were superior, but what did that matter? All this, they said, had been foreseen and discounted. . . .

Even when she was winning, her civilian statesmen, her High Command, and her soldiers, repeated that this was no contest between armaments; it was a pitting of our faith in things against their faith in spirit.[55]

November 25, 1970 was chosen as the day that Mishima would fulfill his destiny as a Samurai, pitting his faith in spirit against the modern era. Four others from the *Tatenokai* joined him. All donned headbands bearing a *Hagakure* slogan. The aim was to take General Mashida hostage to enable Mishima to address the soldiers stationed at the Ichigaya army base in Tokyo. Mishima and his lieutenant, Masakatsu Morita, would then commit *hara-kiri*. Only daggers and swords would be used in the assault, in accordance with Samurai tradition.[56]

The General was bound and gagged. Close fighting ensued as officers several times entered the general's office. Mishima and his small band each time forced the officers to retreat. Finally, they were herded out with broad strokes of Mishima's sword against their buttocks. A thousand soldiers assembled on the parade ground. Two of Mishima's men dropped leaflets from the balcony above, calling for a rebellion to "restore Nippon."

Precisely at mid-day, Mishima appeared on the balcony to address the crowd. Shouting above the noise of helicopters he declared: "Japanese people today think of money, just money: Where is our national spirit today? The *Jieitai*[57] must be the soul of Japan."

The soldiers jeered. Mishima continued: "The nation has no spiritual foundation. That is why you don't agree with me. You will just be American mercenaries. There you are in your tiny

---

[55] Benedict, p. 21.
[56] Stokes, pp. 29–51.
[57] Army.

world. You do nothing for Japan." His last words were: "I salute the Emperor. Long live the Emperor!"

Morita joined him on the balcony in salute.

Both returned to Mashida's office. Mishima knelt, shouting a final salute, and plunged a dagger into his stomach, forcing it clockwise. Morita bungled the decapitation leaving it for another to finish. Morita was then handed Mishima's dagger but called upon the swordsman who had finished off Mishima to do the job, and Morita's head was knocked off in one swoop. The remaining followers stood the heads of Mishima and Morita together and prayed over them.

Ten thousand mourners attended Mishima's funeral, the largest of its kind ever held in Japan.[58] "I want to make a poem of my life," Mishima had written at the age of twenty-four. He had fulfilled his destiny according to the Samurai way: "To choose the place where one dies is also the greatest joy in life." Mishima wrote in his commentary on *Hagakure*: "The positive form of suicide called *hara-kiri* is not a sign of defeat, as it is in the West, but the ultimate expression of free will, in order to protect one's honor."[59]

After his death, his commentary on *Hagakure* became an immediate best-seller.[60]

Counter-Currents/*North American New Right*
January 14, 2011

---

[58] Stokes, p. 241.
[59] *Mishima on Hagakure*, p. 46.
[60] Kathryn Sparling, "Translator's Note," p. vii.

INDEX

A
Ackroyd, Peter, 45, 55, 77
agrarianism, 64–65
Aiwass, 30, 32
Aldington, Richard, 148
Amaudruz, Guy, 153
anarchism, 5, 9, 12, 17, 21, 27, 32, 34, 41, 80, 81, 103
anti-Semitism, 16, 46, 68, 77, 97–100, 139, 140
Apollo, 21, 137, 142
aristocracy, 19, 29, 33, 34, 44, 53, 55, 73, 104, 132, 133, 160
Australia, 79, 80, 82, 84–102

B
Babbitt, Irving, 55, 61
Bakunin, Mikhail, 5–14, 16, 18, 25, 80, 81, 82
Baldwin, Stanley, 81, 142
Balzac, Honoré de, 86
Baudelaire, Charles, 116
Bayreuth Festival, 23–25
Bedford, 12th Duke of, 143–44, 145
Beethoven, Ludwig van, 5
Belloc, Hillaire, 48, 77
Benedict, Ruth, 158, 160, 166, 172
Bielicki, Richard, 147
Bioncourt, Countess de, 146
Binet, Ren, 153
Bismarck, Otto von, 24
Blake, William, 109, 116, 124, 149
Bloomsbury Group, 52, 62, 105, 130, 138
Bolshevism, 48, 64, 69, 82, 88, 145, 150

Bose, Subhas Chandra, 145
British Union of Fascists, 42, 141, 142, 153
Bullock, Laurence, 100 n61
Burns, Robert, 86
Buruma, Ian, 160

C
Campbell, Eric, 91 n45
Campbell, Roy, 60, 64, 80, 105, 139, 148
capitalism (see also: money power, usury), 1, 2, 40, 44, 51, 52, 64, 66, 69, 81, 95, 108, 119, 146, 165
Carlyle, Thomas, 21
Chamberlin, Houston Stewart, 19, 24
Charlemagne, 125–26
Chaucer, Geoffrey, 86
Chekhov, Anton, 86
Christianity, 22, 26, 30, 42, 51–54, 68, 76, 82, 109, 142
Clark, Helen, 132 n16
class, 1, 3, 8, 14, 15, 20, 24, 29, 32, 36, 60, 66, 70, 71, 72, 73, 76, 77, 95, 108, 123, 138, 154, 158, 171.
classicism, 55–57, 113
Clune, Frank, 101–102
Coleridge, Samuel Taylor, 116
Communism (see also: Marxism), 1, 14–15, 21, 27, 43, 52, 53, 62, 81, 91, 94, 95, 104, 108, 111, 120, 133, 139, 140, 165
corporatism, 28, 30, 46, 71, 107, 107 n39, 161, 180
Cresswell, D'arcy, 129

Crowley, Aleister, iii, 26–43, 83–84, 97
culture, 6, 16, 17, 19, 22, 34, 35, 37, 38, 44, 47, 50, 53, 54, 57–61, 63, 64, 67, 70–78, 85–88, 103, 106–108, 110, 112–20
Curnow, Allen, 127, 129, 135
cyclical history, 43, 47, 87, 106, 107, 122, 172

D
D'Annunzio, Gabriele, 40–41
Dale, A. S., 52
Darwinism, 33
De Lozey, Leslie, 137–38
democracy, 1, 6, 7, 19, 21, 26, 29, 30, 32, 34, 35, 36, 40–41, 42, 47, 64, 69–70, 73, 89, 92, 93, 95, 96, 129, 134, 136, 141, 142, 147, 154–55, 158, 162, 167, 169, 170
Dickens, Charles, 86
Distributism, 43
Dobree, Bonamy, 54
Dollfuss, Engelbert, 40
Dostoevsky, Fyodor, 86
Douglas, Clifford Hugh (see also: Social Credit), 48, 97, 103, 107, 110 n30, 112, 134

E
economics, see: Social Credit, usury
egalitarianism, see: equality
Edward VIII, 141
Eliot, T. S., 44–78, 96, 107, 111, 138, 140
Elizabeth II, 150
Engdahl, Per, 153
equality, 2, 16, 27, 29, 35, 36, 47, 54, 55, 56, 72, 73, 96, 131, 155
Evola, Julius, 1, 26, 29, 30, 33, 35, 36, 40, 43, 68, 131, 140, 145 n69, 159

F
Fairburn, Rex, 13, 44, 71, 79, 87, 97, 103–28, 129, 130, 133–36, 137, 143 n62, 152
fascism, 41, 42, 52, 53, 57, 61, 62, 64, 67, 68, 69, 71, 76, 129, 140, 141, 147–52, 156
feminism, 95, 103, 126–28
feudalism, 1, 160, 165
Feuerbach, Ludwig, 21
Fichte, J. G., 2, 4, 8
Firth, Clifton, 109
Fleming, Greig, 130, 156
Fowler, R. G., 148 n75
freedom, 12, 14, 18, 19, 21, 33, 35, 43, 110, 122, 134, 154, 167, 170
Freemasonry, 26, 27, 28
Frederick II, Barbarossa, 3–4
French Revolution, 2, 21, 27, 56, 69
Freudianism, 127
Frost, Robert, 77
Fuller, J. F. C., 42
Futurism, 58 n38, 68

G
Gandhi, Mohandas, 145
Glass, Douglas, 137–38
Glover, Dennis, 127
Gobineau, Count Arthur de, 3, 16, 24
Goering, Hermann, 147
Goethe, Johann Wolfgang von, 74, 86
Golden Dawn, Hermetic Order of, 28, 30
Goldston, Edward, 97
Gorky, Maxim, 86
Gramsci, Antonio, 24
Greece, Ancient, 22, 162

Index 177

Great Depression, 129
Guénon, René, 26, 27, 29, 30, 33
guilds, 36, 39, 40, 62, 71, 73, 107
guild socialism, 36, 73

H
Hamilton, Alastair, 47
Hamsun, Knut, 50, 67, 71, 79, 86, 106, 156
Hann, George, 141
Hegel, G. W. F., 5, 8, 11, 21, 86
Heine, Heinrich, 7, 86
Herder, Johann Gottfried, 2, 3, 4, 8
Herzen, Alexander, 81
Heseltine, Nigel, 141
hierarchy, 38, 103, 154, 172
Hitler, Adolf, 50, 52, 69, 98, 140, 141, 143, 144, 147
homosexuality, 105, 130
Horus, 26, 31, 33, 43
Hugo, Victor, 86
Hulme, T. E., 55
Huxley, Aldous, 137, 139
Hyde, Robin, 112

I
Ibsen, Henrik, 86
Illuminati, 26–27, 41
individualism, 31, 32, 34, 57, 103, 107, 119, 134 n24
industrialism, 1, 26, 35, 55, 63, 64, 70, 108
Ingamells, Rex, 89, 94

J
Jesus, 6–7, 82
Jewish Question, the, 4 n8, 7, 8, 10–11, 12, 16, 17, 18, 19, 48–51, 90, 97, 98, 99, 115–16, 140
John, Augustus, 137
Jordan, Colin, 148, 152, 153
Joyce, William (Lord Haw Haw), 141, 147, 153
Julian the Apostate, 142
Julius Caesar, 137
Jung, Carl Gustav, 158, 160

K
Kant, Immanuel, 4, 86
Katyn Massacre, 142–45
Kawabata, Yasunari, 166
Kipling, Rudyard, 119
Klossowski, Andrzej, 156
Krakouer, Nancy, 100 n61
Kropotkin, Peter, 18

L
Lane, William, 99
Lang, Jack, 91 n45
Lawrence, David Herbert, 51, 64, 70, 79, 83, 103, 107, 109, 170
Lawson, Henry, 86, 99
Lee, John A., 110 n30
Leese, Arnold, 142
Lenin, V. I., 27 n1, 81, 109
Lévi, Éliphas (Alphonse Louis Constant), 27, 29, 30, 32
Lewis, Wyndham, 42, 55, 62, 113, 133, 140, 141
liberalism, 17, 19, 26, 27, 34, 46, 47, 50, 54, 62, 67, 69, 70, 72, 88, 103
liberty, see: freedom
Luburić, Vjekoslav, 153–54
Ludwig II, King of Bavaria, 14, 19, 23

M
MacGregor Mathers, Samuel Liddell, 28
Machiavelli, Niccolò, 2
Mallarmé, Stéphane, 116
Mansfield, Katherine, 107
Marinetti, Filippo, 68

Martin, Chris, 146, 157
Marx, Karl, 1–2, 10, 11, 43, 44, 71, 108
Marxism (see also: Communism), 3, 40, 44, 94, 103, 108, 127, 129, 134
Mason, R. A. K., 103, 108, 110, 115, 127, 132, 135, 136, 152
mass society, 64
Maurras, Charles, 53, 55, 56, 57, 62, 156
McAlpine, J., 62
McCahon, Colin, 114
McLeish, Archibald, 77
mechanization, 64, 68
Mendelsohn, Felix, 115
Mickiewicz, Adam, 146, 156
Miles, W. J., 83, 88, 89
Mishima, Yukio, 158–74
Mishita, General, 173, 174
monarchism, 56
money power (See also: capitalism, usury), 47
Montalk, Stephanie, 135, 138, 139, 146 n69, 147, 149, 152
Montrose, 7th Duke of (James Graham), 150
Morita, Masakatsu, 173–74
Mosley, Sir Oswald, 42, 93, 141, 142, 145 n69
Mountain, Guy, 109
Mudie, Ian, 89, 100, 101
Muirden, Bruce, 79 n2, 88, 100
Mussolini, Benito, 40, 41, 42, 52, 61, 91 n45, 137

N
National Socialism, 16, 24, 93, 94, 104, 141
nationalism, 2, 4, 12, 54, 67, 68, 72, 83, 93, 95, 102, 111, 115, 116, 117
Nietzsche, Friedrich, 26, 30, 32, 33, 80–83, 107
Nitobe, Inazo, 159–60

O
Orage, Alfred Richard, 37, 48. 62, 73, 106–107, 134
Orwell, George, 37, 48, 63, 73, 107, 134

P
pacifism, 169–70
paganism, 133, 142
Pater, Walter, 116
Pétain, Philippe, 53 n24
Picasso, Pablo, 112, 113
Potocki, Geoffrey (Count Potocki of Montalk), 44, 104, 105, 127, 129–57
Potocki, Odile, 142, 145
Potocki, Peter, 157
Pound, Ezra, 44, 45, 46, 47, 48, 50, 51, 55, 57, 60, 61, 63, 64, 70, 77, 78, 79, 96, 97, 107, 111–12, 113, 120, 122, 129, 133, 138, 147 n72, 156
Proudhon, Pierre Joseph, 9–10, 16, 21, 25
Puritanism, 142, 154

Q
Quicke, E. C., 100 n61

R
Rabelais, François, 86, 137
race, 3, 16, 25, 35, 50, 65, 85–86, 88, 140–41, 149
reactionaries, 1, 11, 52, 61, 68, 69, 140
Read, Herbert, 45
Regardie, Israel, 83, 97
Remer, Otto Ernst, 146 n69
Roman Empire, 22
romanticism, 8, 55–57

Rothschild family, 11, 16
Roosevelt, Franklin Delano, 72
Rousseau, Jean-Jacques, 6, 55–56, 96
Russell, Bertrand, 137

S
Salazar, Antonio, 40
Savitri Devi, 132 n11, 148
Shakespeare, William, 74, 86
Slavs, 5, 7, 11
Social Credit, 42–43, 47–48, 51, 57, 63, 73, 96, 97, 103, 104, 106–12, 122, 124, 125, 129, 134
socialism (see also: Communism, guild socialism, Marxism, National Socialism), 1, 2, 10, 14, 15, 42, 51, 52, 56–57, 81, 93, 94, 104, 133, 134, 170
Soddy, Frederick, 62
Sorel, Georges, 56, 57
Spengler, Oswald, 1, 44, 47, 60, 87, 103, 106, 107, 108, 122, 124, 134, 168, 171–72
Stalin, Joseph, 115 n45, 151
Stephensen, Percy Reginald, iii, 79–102, 128, 149 n80
Stern, Fritz, 47
Stokes, Henry Scott, 164–65 n24
Strasser, Otto, 145 n69
syndicalism, 36, 40, 41, 43, 56

T
Tashiro, 167
technology, 74, 77, 161
Tito, Josip Broz, 154
Tolstoy, Leo, 86
Traditionalism (school), 26–30, 36, 39, 159
Trotsky, Leon, 81
Trussell, Denys, 112, 117, 120, 124

U
usury (see also money power), 7, 24, 47, 63, 71, 120–22, 134

V
Van Aelst, Heather, 59
Verlaine, Paul, 137
Viereck, Peter, 18, 20 n49
vitalism, 8, 107
Voltaire, 86
Vorticism, 113

W
Wagner, Richard, 1–25, 86
Walsh, Adele Pankhurst, 90, 91 n46
Walsh, Tom, 91
Watts, Dora, 100–101 n65
Watts, Martin, 100
Weishaupt, Adam, 27, 29, 32 n30
West, Mae, 125
West, Rebecca, 137
Westcott, William Wynn, 28
Wild, Sir Ernest, 137
Wilde, Oscar, 104, 110, 134
Wilson, R. McNair, 63
Wodehouse, P. G., 156
Wolfe, Humbert, 115
Wren, Christopher, 54
Wright, F. W. Nielsen, 155, 156

Y
Yamamoto, Jocho, 167–72
Yeats, William Butler, 28, 35, 42, 60, 64, 68, 70, 104, 109, 133, 137, 138, 159
Yockey, Francis Parker (Ulick Varange), 145 n69

Z
Zachary, G. Pascal, 66, 118 n53
Zukofsky, Lewis, 77

About the Author

K. R. Bolton holds Doctorates in Theology and a Ph.D. h.c. He is a contributing writer for *Foreign Policy Journal* and a Fellow of the Academy of Social and Political Research in Greece.

His books include *Revolution from Above* (London: Arktos Media, 2011), *Artists of the Right* (San Francisco: Counter-Currents, 2012), *Stalin: The Enduring Legacy* (London: Black House Publishing, 2012), *The Parihaka Cult* (London: Black House Publishing, 2012), *The Psychotic Left* (London: Black House Publishing, 2013), *The Banking Swindle: Money Creation and the State* (London: Black House Publishing, 2013), *Babel Inc.: Multicultralism, Globalisation, and the New World Order* (London: Black House Publishing, 2014), *Perón and Perónism* (London: Black House Publishing, 2014), and *Zionism, Islam, and the West* (London: Black House Publishing, 2015).

His articles have been published by both scholarly and popular media, including the *International Journal of Social Economics*; *Journal of Social, Political, and Economic Studies*; *Geopolitika*; *World Affairs*; *India Quarterly*; *The Occidental Quarterly*; *North American New Right*; Radio Free Asia; *Irish Journal of Gothic & Horror Studies*, Trinity College; *International Journal of Russian Studies*, and many others.

His writings have been translated into French, German, Russian, Italian, Czech, Latvian, Persian, and Vietnamese.

www.ingramcontent.com/pod-product-compliance
Lightning Source LLC
Chambersburg PA
CBHW031320160426
43196CB00007B/597